BIKING OHIO'S
RAIL-TRAILS

OTHER BOOKS BY
SHAWN E. RICHARDSON

Biking USA's Rail-Trails
Biking Missouri's Rail-Trails
Biking Wisconsin's Rail-Trails

BIKING OHIO'S
RAIL-TRAILS

Where to Go • What to Expect • How to Get There

by
SHAWN E. RICHARDSON

ADVENTURE PUBLICATIONS, INC.
Cambridge, MN

ADVENTURE PUBLICATIONS, INC.
820 Cleveland St. S
Cambridge, MN 55008
1-800-678-7006

BIKING OHIO'S RAIL-TRAILS
Where to Go, What to Expect, How to Get There

Seventh Printing
Copyright 2000 by Shawn E. Richardson. All rights Reserved.
Revised 2002

ISBN: 1-885061-86-2

Text, research, cartography and photography by Shawn E. Richardson. The photograph for the Great Ohio Lake to River Greenway is by Kevin Grippi.

Edited by Dr. Harold E. Richardson

Front cover:
    Central photo: The Little Miami Scenic Trail near Yellow Springs, Ohio.
    Inset photo: The National Road Bikeway Tunnel in St. Clairsville, Ohio.

Back cover:
    Top: The Towpath Trail, a section of the Ohio to Erie Trail, follows the
        Old Ohio-Erie Canal.
    Middle: A scene along the Emerald Necklace Trail near Lakewood.
    Bottom: The Towpath Trail, a section of the Ohio to Erie Trail, traverses
        wetlands as a boardwalk.

This book is for Dr. Harold Edward and Antonia Calvert Richardson, Jill C. Richardson Lang, Tom Edwards and Mary Gleason Boone, Tom Edwards Boone Jr., Betsy Boone-Abraham, Steven M. Slucher, Tina Davy, Mark J. Ballenger, Rob G. Koenig, Henry Christain Herrmann III, Tom and Susan Mc Feely, Kathaleen Mc Feeley, Ryan Mc Feeley, Dean Focke and my wife Joyce A. Richardson for joining me in trail blazing across Ohio's rail-trails.

A special thanks goes to Terry Berrigan and Seneca Murley of the Ohio Field Office of the Rails-to-Trails Conservancy for keeping my research information updated and accurate. A special thanks also goes to Ed Honton of the Ohio-to-Erie Trail Coalition for keeping me updated with the latest happenings of the 335-mile cross-state trail.

A special thanks also goes to the recreationalists who will use these trails.

CONTENTS

INTRODUCTION

I researched and created Biking Ohio's Rail-Trails as a guide to Ohio's major off-road multi-purpose trails and rail-trails. It provides tourists, weekend travelers, outdoor lovers and recreationalists with a set of uniform, detailed maps that allow them to easily find each trail. The maps and text also help drivers find parking and other locations to drop off or pick up trail users. Maps of trails with permanent mile markers help users calculate the distance of their outdoor excursions.

Most of the trails described herein have a smooth surface to allow users to bicycle, mountain bicycle, walk, hike, or travel by wheelchair. Many are opened to cross-country skiers during the winter months, and some even allow horseback riding. Best of all, Ohio prohibits motorized vehicles from using the trails at any time, providing a safe alternative to users throughout the year. Check each individual trail to make sure it allows for your intended use.

While the book does not include maps for many of the shorter or limited use trails, a description of each trail can be found under "Ohio's Limited Use Rail-Trails" on page 156, and Ohio's Minor Bike Trails on Page 160.

The maps and information in Biking Ohio's Rail-Trails are current as of 2002. Future editions will include trails currently under development, a list of which appears under "Ohio's Potential Rail-Trails" on page 168. If you find that any of the maps need corrections, or if you have discovered trails not listed, write to me in care of Biking U.S.A.'s Rail-Trails, P.O. Box 284, Hilliard, OH 43026-0284. I hope this book makes trail blazing across the Buckeye State more convenient and enjoyable for you, and whenever you use these trails, always keep in mind the safety tips listed in the back of this book. Happy Trails!

– Shawn E. Richardson, 2002

Shawn E. Richardson's e-mail address
shawnerichardson@yahoo.com

Visit his web page!!!
http://www.BikingUSARailTrails.com

THE RAILS-TO-TRAILS CONSERVANCY

Founded in 1985 with the mission of enhancing America's communities and countryside, the Rails-to-Trails Conservancy is a national nonprofit organization dedicated to converting abandoned rail corridors into a nationwide network of multi-purpose trails. By linking parks, schools, neighborhoods, communities, towns, cities, states and national parks, this system will connect important landmarks and create both a haven for wildlife and a safe place for everyone to bicycle, walk, in-line skate and travel by wheelchair. Rail-trails meet demands for local recreational opportunities and connect with long-distance trails to make it possible to ride continuously across a state and eventually from coast to coast without encountering a motorized vehicle. For more information, contact the Rails-to-Trails Conservancy, 1100 17th St. NW, 10th Floor, Washington, D.C. 20036 or call 202-331-9696.

Biking USA's Rail-Trails (Book and Website)

A handy reference for finding rail-trails across the country is the book **Biking USA's Rail-Trails**, also by Shawn E. Richardson. This guide provides tourists, weekend travelers, outdoor enthusiasts and recreationalists with information about the USA's major multi-purpose trails and rail-trails. State locator maps show where the major trails are, and information such as surface type, trail length, trail use and more is provided for each trail.

The Biking USA's Rail-Trails website is a companion to the book, and was designed to promote and provide information about the most prominent and scenic rail-trails across the country. The website gives examples of rail-to-trail, highway-to-bikeway and towpath-to-bikepath conversions. Under "trails and photos," mileage charts, a locator map USA's top rail-trails, and pictures from nearly every state are shown. Fun and games with questions and puzzles relating to rail-trails can be enjoyed under "rail-trail trivia." Of course, all of the answers can be found in **Biking USA's Rail-Trails**.

TRAIL DESCRIPTIONS

ASPHALT OR CONCRETE-suitable for bicycling, mountain bicycling, hiking, in-line skating and wheelchairs.

COARSE ASPHALT-suitable for bicycling, mountain bicycling, hiking and wheelchairs.

SMOOTH CRUSHED GRAVEL-suitable for bicycling, mountain bicycling, hiking and wheelchairs. During thawing and extremely wet weather, bicycles, mountain bicycles and wheelchairs should avoid using this trail surface since the soft surface can rut easily.

COARSE CRUSHED GRAVEL-suitable for mountain bicycling and hiking.

GRASS OR DIRT-suitable for mountain bicycling and hiking.

ORIGINAL BALLAST-difficult for most trail users due to the size of larger rocks.

NOTE: Trail users should check conditions for each trail by contacting the trail managers listed in this book.

LEGEND

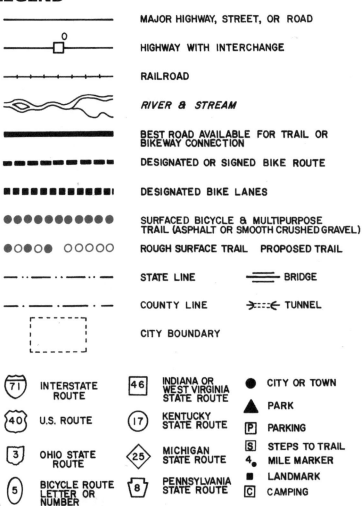

————————	MAJOR HIGHWAY, STREET, OR ROAD
	HIGHWAY WITH INTERCHANGE
—+—+—+—+—	RAILROAD
	RIVER & STREAM
▬▬▬▬▬▬▬▬	BEST ROAD AVAILABLE FOR TRAIL OR BIKEWAY CONNECTION
▬ ▬ ▬ ▬ ▬ ▬ ▬ ▬	DESIGNATED OR SIGNED BIKE ROUTE
■■■■■■■■■■	DESIGNATED BIKE LANES
●●●●●●●●●●	SURFACED BICYCLE & MULTIPURPOSE TRAIL (ASPHALT OR SMOOTH CRUSHED GRAVEL)
●○●○● ○○○○○	ROUGH SURFACE TRAIL PROPOSED TRAIL
— ·· — · — ·· —	STATE LINE ═══ BRIDGE
— · — · — · —	COUNTY LINE ≻∷∷∶← TUNNEL
⌐ ¬	CITY BOUNDARY

(71)	INTERSTATE ROUTE	[46]	INDIANA OR WEST VIRGINIA STATE ROUTE	●	CITY OR TOWN
{40}	U.S. ROUTE	(17)	KENTUCKY STATE ROUTE	▲	PARK
				[P]	PARKING
[3]	OHIO STATE ROUTE	◇25◇	MICHIGAN STATE ROUTE	[S]	STEPS TO TRAIL
				4.	MILE MARKER
(5)	BICYCLE ROUTE LETTER OR NUMBER	⑧	PENNSYLVANIA STATE ROUTE	■	LANDMARK
				[C]	CAMPING

TRAIL USERS SYMBOLS:
B = BICYCLES
H = HORSES
M = MOUNTAIN BICYCLES
R = ROLLERBLADING / SKATING
W = WALKING / JOGGING
X = CROSS COUNTRY SKIING
WH = WHEEL CHAIR USERS

TRAIL USE SYMBOLS

Dark symbols: trail use allowed. Light symbols: trail use not allowed

🚲	Bicycling	🚵	Mountain Bicycling
🚶	Hiking	⛸	In-line Skating
🏇	Bridal Path	⛷	Cross-Country Skiing
♿	Handicap Accessible		

STATE MAP SHOWING OHIO'S TRAILS

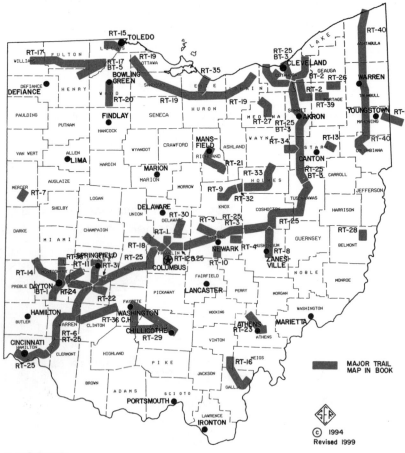

LEGEND

RT: MAJOR RAIL-TRAIL
(greater than 1 mile and/or smooth surface trail following a former railroad)

BT: BIKE TRAIL
(smooth surface trail not following a former railroad)

OHIO'S TRAILS

HELP KEEP US UPDATED

Are there any new bike trails in your area? Did we not list a major bike trail which should have been included in this book? Have any trails listed in this book gone through any changes? Whether the trail has changed in length, surface, types of trail use, address, phone number, web page address or even the trail name itself, we would like to know so you can help us keep this publication accurate and up to date.

Please copy this page, answer the questions, and send it to Biking Ohio's Rail-Trails, P.O. Box 284, Hilliard, OH 43026. This will help us give our trailblazers the best and most accurate information for biking Ohio's rail-trails.

Exact Trail name

Was any part of this trail formerly a railroad?

Vicinity? City (Street or spot) to City (Street or spot)

Trail Length (miles)?

Trail Surface?   (concrete, asphalt, smooth crushed gravel)

Trail Use? (Yes or No)
Bicycle_____ Cross Country Skiing_____ Mountain Bicycle_____
Snowmobile_____ Walking-Hiking_____ Wheelchair Use_____ Roller Skating or
Roller Blades_____ ATV Use_____ Golf Cart Use_____ Horseback riding_____
Trail Users Fee_____ Horse & Buggy or Horse & Wagon_____

Address for Trail Information?

Phone Number for Trail Information?

Web Page for Trail?

Is the trail smooth enough for a touring bicycle?

When (Year) was the trail (First Section) built/open?

To make our research easier, could you provide us a map of the trail showing mile posts and parking spots?

Are there any other adjacent bike trails near by?

Are there any local bicycle route guide maps of your area? If so, where could we find them?

Any other comments?

Please answer these questions completely and send this page to the address above. Thanks for you input.

OHIO'S MAJOR RAIL-TRAILS

OLENTANGY/LOWER SCIOTO BIKEWAYS (Bike Route-47)

VICINITY: *Columbus*
TRAIL LENGTH: *20.2 miles*
SURFACE: *Asphalt/Concrete*
TRAIL USE: 🚴 🚲 🚶 🏕 🐎 ⛷ ♿

Constructed in 1967, Ohio's first rail-trail, the Lower Scioto Bikeway ran 1.5 miles between Frank Road and Greenlawn Avenue as it followed an abandoned railroad corridor along the west bank of the Scioto River. In the following years, other sections of the bikeway were built north along both the Scioto River and the Olentangy River. Bicyclists enter the south end of the bikeway from a 50-foot dirt path accessible on Frank Road (State Route-104). The bikeway traverses Columbus from the south end to the north end before proceeding north to Worthington. Many sections of Ohio's oldest trail suffer from outdated standards such as sharp curves, narrow bridges and narrow urban sidewalks near Greenlawn Avenue; however, users will find most of the trail very scenic and pleasant to travel. Use extreme caution in congested areas. The more experienced cyclists can follow the Bike Route-49 signs along Front Street through German Village and downtown Columbus, then along Neil Avenue through the Short North neighborhood and O.S.U. Campus Area as an alternative route.

Please note that the bike path has been under long term construction between State Route-315 and Grandview Avenue with the improvements of Dublin Road (US Route-33).

The skyline of Columbus, Ohio along the Olentangy and Lower Scioto Bikeways.

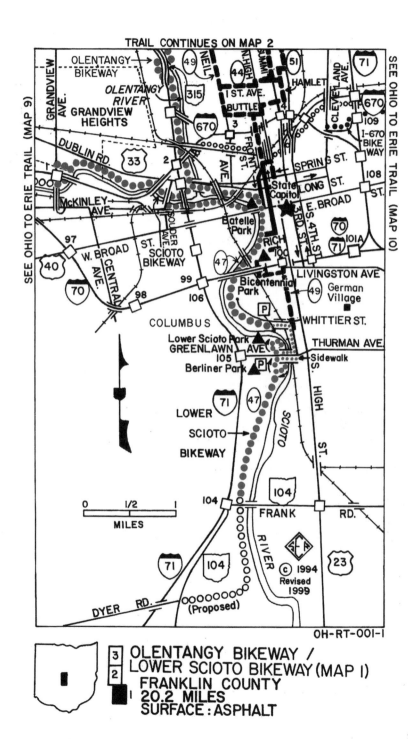

TRAIL CONTINUES ON MAP 2

OLENTANGY BIKEWAY

OLENTANGY RIVER

GRANDVIEW HEIGHTS

GRANDVIEW AVE.

SEE OHIO TO ERIE TRAIL (MAP 9)

NEIL

44

SUMMIT

N.HIGH

51

HAMLET

1 ST. AVE.

BUTTLE

3

315

670

FRONT ST.

CLEVELAND AVE.

71

670

109

I-670 BIKEWAY

108

SEE OHIO TO ERIE TRAIL (MAP 10)

DUBLIN RD.

33

2

SPRING ST.

LONG ST.

State Capitol

McKINLEY AVE.

GOLDEN AVE.

Batelle Park

3RD ST.

S. 4TH ST.

E. BROAD

70

71

101A

97

40

70

W. BROAD AVE.

CENTRAL AVE.

ST.

SCIOTO BIKEWAY

99

47

RICH

100

LIVINGSTON AVE

106

98

Bicentennial Park

49

German Village

COLUMBUS

Lower Scioto Park

GREENLAWN AVE.

105

Berliner Park

P

P

WHITTIER ST.

THURMAN AVE.

Sidewalk

S. HIGH ST.

Scioto

71

47

LOWER

SCIOTO→

BIKEWAY

0   1/2   1
MILES

104

104

FRANK

RD.

71

104

RIVER

S-F-A

© 1994
Revised
1999

23

DYER RD.

(Proposed)

OH-RT-001-1

OLENTANGY BIKEWAY /
LOWER SCIOTO BIKEWAY (MAP I)
FRANKLIN COUNTY
20.2 MILES
SURFACE: ASPHALT

3

Highlights along these trails include German Village, the State Capitol, downtown Columbus, the Santa Maria, the Confluence, Ohio State University, Whetstone Park of Roses, Antrim Lake, the center of Old Worthington and numerous city parks. The most popular spot along the Olentangy Bikeway is the lake at Antrim Park, which offers wonderful scenery and a special loop trail around the lake for walkers and joggers. Another popular and scenic spot along the same trail is the Whetstone Park of Roses.

The Columbus Recreation and Parks Department has plans for extensions, connections and improvements for the two bikeways in the near future. Contact them for current information.

Mark J. Ballenger uses his bicycle and passenger trailer for biking Ohio's trails while book author Shawn E. Richardson takes a back seat (Antrim Lake).

PARKING:
Antrim Park offers the best spot to find a parking space along the trail, and parking is also available in the Whetstone Park of Roses.

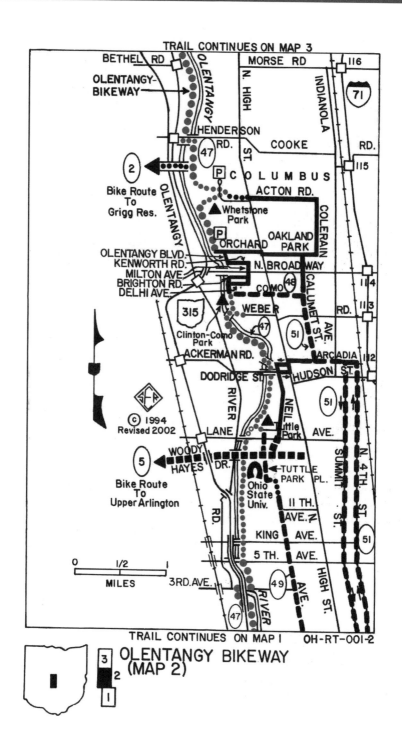

TRAIL CONTINUES ON MAP 3

OLENTANGY-BIKEWAY

BETHEL RD.

OLENTANGY

MORSE RD.

116

N. HIGH ST.

INDIANOLA

71

HENDERSON RD.

COOKE

RD.

47

115

2

Bike Route To Grigg Res.

P COLUMBUS

ACTON RD.

OLENTANGY

COLERAIN

Whetstone Park

P OAKLAND PARK

ORCHARD

OLENTANGY BLVD.
KENWORTH RD.
MILTON AVE.
BRIGHTON RD.
DELHI AVE.

N. BROADWAY

COMO 48

CALUMET ST.

114

315

WEBER

RD. 113

Clinton-Como Park

47

51

ACKERMAN RD.

ARCADIA 112

DODRIDGE ST.

HUDSON ST.

RIVER

NEIL AVE.

51

© 1994
Revised 2002

Tuttle Park

LANE

AVE.

SUMMIT ST.

5

WOODY HAYES DR.

TUTTLE PARK PL.

N. 4TH ST.

Bike Route To Upper Arlington

Ohio State Univ.

11 TH. AVE. Z

RD.

KING AVE.

51

5 TH. AVE.

0   1/2   1
MILES

3RD. AVE.

49

RIVER

HIGH ST.

AVE.

47

TRAIL CONTINUES ON MAP 1

OH-RT-001-2

3
2
1

OLENTANGY BIKEWAY (MAP 2)

The oldest rail-trail in Ohio is between State Route-104 and Greenlawn Avenue.

Ohio's State Capitol, Columbus, Ohio.

FOR MORE INFORMATION:

Columbus Recreation and Parks Dept.
200 Greenlawn Ave., Columbus, OH 43223
614-645-3308

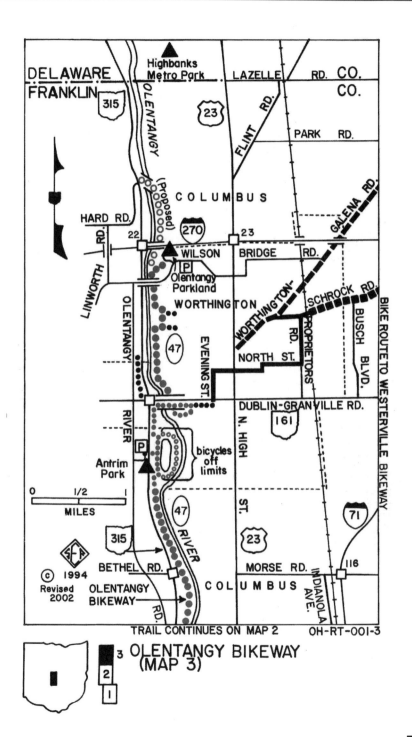

DELAWARE
FRANKLIN

315

Highbanks
Metro Park

LAZELLE   RD. CO.
                    CO.

23

FLINT   RD.

PARK   RD.

OLENTANGY

(Proposed)

C O L U M B U S

HARD RD.

270

23

22

WILSON   BRIDGE   RD.

P
Olentangy
Parkland

GALENA RD.

LINWORTH   RD.

OLENTANGY

WORTHINGTON

47

EVENING ST.

WORTHINGTON-

SCHROCK RD.

PROPRIETORS   RD.

BUSCH   BLVD.

BIKE ROUTE TO WESTERVILLE BIKEWAY

NORTH ST.

RIVER

DUBLIN-GRANVILLE RD.

161

P

Antrim
Park

bicycles
off
limits

N. HIGH

ST.

0   1/2   1
MILES

47

71

315

RIVER

23

SFA

© 1994

Revised
2002

BETHEL   RD.

MORSE RD.

116

OLENTANGY
BIKEWAY

C O L U M B U S

INDIANOLA AVE.

RD.

TRAIL CONTINUES ON MAP 2   OH-RT-001-3

3 OLENTANGY BIKEWAY
    (MAP 3)

2
1

BIKE & HIKE TRAIL

VICINITY: *Cleveland/Akron/Kent*
TRAIL LENGTH: *29.0 Miles*
SURFACE: *Asphalt and Smooth Crushed Gravel*
TRAIL USE: 🚲 🏍️ 🚶 🐎 ⛸️ 🚶 (🚃 *between Silver Lake and Kent*)

The Ohio Edison Company and the Metroparks joined forces in 1972 to create the Bike and Hike Trail, and since that time Ohio's second rail-trail has been used as a model for similar efforts across the United States. Much of the path, which follows two old railroad grades and a former interurban electric railroad line, traverses the northern part of Summit County between Cleveland, Akron and Kent. Highlights include the Emerald Necklace, Brandywine Falls, Virginia Kendall Park (N.P.S.), Silver Springs Park and the Cuyahoga River

A scenic cut in the Bike and Hike Trail near Boston Heights.

While most of the trail has a smooth, screened limestone surface, two sections have been covered with asphalt. The first of these paved paths parallels State Route-8 near Cuyahoga Falls while the second runs from Cuyahoga Falls to Kent. Streets marked with "bike route" signs connect sections of the trail through Cuyahoga Falls. The most tranquil part of the trail lies between the Ohio Turnpike (Interstate-80) and State Route-303 where it runs through several deep railroad cuts with rock ledges on each side. Other spots along the trail have very high fills that provide trail users with a splendid view of the woods below.

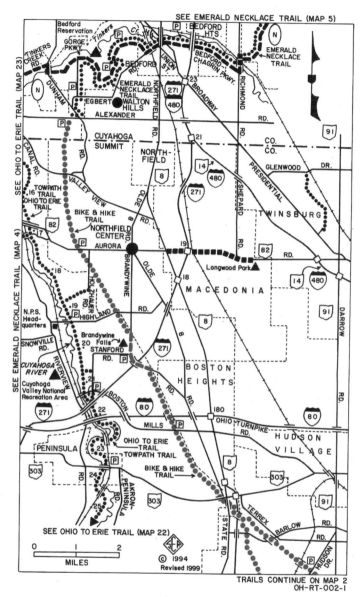

SEE EMERALD NECKLACE TRAIL (MAP 5)

TRAILS CONTINUE ON MAP 2
OH-RT-002-1

BIKE & HIKE TRAIL (MAP 1)
CUYAHOGA, SUMMIT, & PORTAGE
COUNTIES
29.0 MILES
SURFACE: ASPHALT & SMOOTH
CRUSHED GRAVEL

This scenic trail connects with two other spectacular multi-purpose trails, the Towpath Trail (also known as the Ohio to Erie Trail) to the west, and the Emerald Necklace Trail, to the north. Cities such as Stow and Munroe Falls also have local bike paths connected to the Bike & Hike Trail. A signed bike route goes through the neighborhoods of Kent from the southeast end of the Bike & Hike Trail to the center of town near the famous Kent State University.

PARKING:
Parking is abundant along most of the trail.

A trail head sign on the Bike & Hike Trail.

FOR MORE INFORMATION:
Akron Metroparks District
975 Treaty Line Rd., Akron, OH 44313
330-867-5111

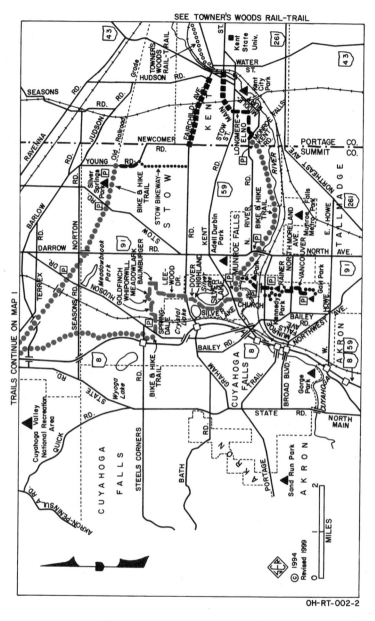

SEE TOWNER'S WOODS RAIL-TRAIL

OH-RT-002-2

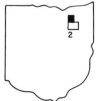

BIKE & HIKE TRAIL (MAP 2)

11

STAVICH BICYCLE TRAIL

VICINITY: *Youngstown*
TRAIL LENGTH: *11.0 Miles*
SURFACE: *Asphalt*
TRAIL USE: 🚴 🚵 🚶 📷 🏇 ⛷ 🚶

The Stavich Bicycle Trail opened in 1983 and follows a former interurban electric railroad grade through three townships, two counties and two states. The trail, constructed and maintained by the families of John and George Stavich, follows the Mahoning River from Struthers, Ohio, to New Castle, Pennsylvania, offering users a vast variety of scenery, including green rolling hills, farmlands and wooded hillsides.

PARKING:

Parking can be found in Struthers along State Route-289 just east of State Route- 616 and along Liberty Street in Lowellville where the trail runs for seven blocks. Parking is also available in New Castle, PA on Washington Street.

The 11-mile bicycle trail parallels the B. & O. Railroad.

FOR MORE INFORMATION:
Falcon Foundry
6th and Water Streets, P.O. Box 301, Lowellville, OH 44436
216-536-6221

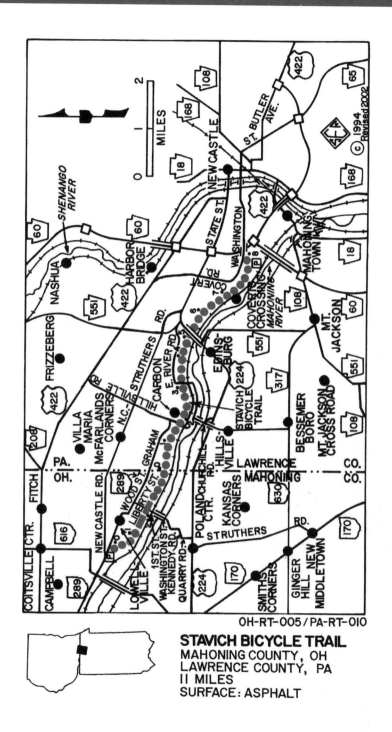

OH-RT-005 / PA-RT-010

STAVICH BICYCLE TRAIL
MAHONING COUNTY, OH
LAWRENCE COUNTY, PA
II MILES
SURFACE: ASPHALT

CELINA-COLDWATER BIKEWAY

VICINITY: *Celina*
TRAIL LENGTH: *4.5 Miles*
SURFACE: *Asphalt*
TRAIL USE: 🚴 🚵 🚶 🏕 🐎 ⛷ ♿

The 4.5-mile Celina-Coldwater Bikeway connects Celina to Coldwater and parallels an active railroad. Well received by both communities it serves, the trail is used by local residents for commuting, socializing and recreating. The trail's scenic rural atmosphere has encouraged many families to enjoy their natural surroundings.

Most of the scenery consists of farmlands, but the main attraction is Grand Lake Saint Mary's, once the largest man-made lake in the world. The Huffy Bicycle Company, headquartered in Celina, purchased the old railroad right-of-way through the Huffy Foundation. Celina, with the help of the Ohio Department of Transportation, secured the construction grant to build the bikeway.

PARKING:
Parking is available in Celina at the corner of Schunk and US Route-127. Parking is also available along Fourth Street in Coldwater.

From left: Author Shawn Richardson, Steve Slucher and Tom Boone get ready to ride.

FOR MORE INFORMATION:
Celina Engineering Dept.
426 W. Market St., Celina, OH 45822
419-586-1144

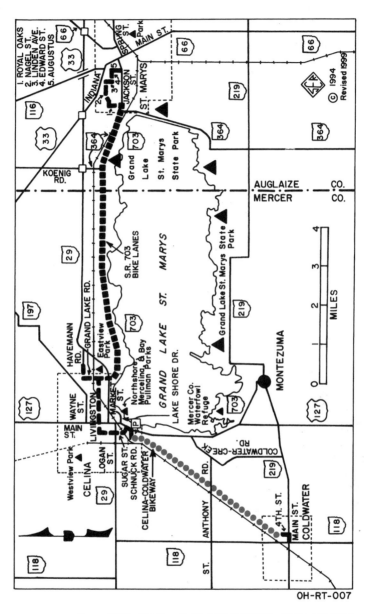

OH-RT-007

CELINA-COLDWATER BIKEWAY
MERCER COUNTY
4.5 MILES
SURFACE: ASPHALT

15

MUSKINGUM RECREATIONAL TRAIL

VICINITY: *Zanesville*
TRAIL LENGTH: *4.5 Miles & 0.5 Miles*
SURFACE: *Asphalt*
TRAIL USE:

ZANE'S LANDING TRAIL

VICINITY: *Zanesville*
TRAIL LENGTH: *3.0 Miles*
SURFACE: *Asphalt*
TRAIL USE:

The 12-mile Muskingum Recreational Trail is in the early planning stages to follow the Muskingum River from Zanesville to Dresden.

When complete, this trail will consist of both asphalt and dirt surfaces for all trail uses including bicycles and horses.

From Market Street in Zanesville, the first three miles of the trail is known as the Zane's Landing Trial, and consists of an asphalt surface. This section of trail takes users from Market Street in downtown Zanesville to Riverview Park in the city's north end. A safety barrier separates the rail-trail from the active railroad it parallels as it follows the Muskingum River north under Interstate-70 to connect with various parks along the river front. An attraction along the trail includes a restored train depot on Market Street near the path's south entrance. The "Lorena," a paddle boat that runs up and down the Muskingum River alongside the bike path, also docks nearby. Zanesville's famous Y-Bridge crosses the Muskingum and Licking Rivers just three blocks south of the old trail depot at Main Street (US Route-40).

From Riverview Park in Zanesville to Dresden, the trail becomes the Muskingum Recreational Trial. Currently, only two sections are open. The first section consists of the trestle over the Muskingum River and can be reached from Ellis. The second section goes from Rock Cut Road north of Ellis to Main Street in Dresden. Parts of this trail also parallel an active railroad separated by woodlands and meadows. Dresden is the home of the famous Longaberger Family Baskets which is the main attraction for visitors. Future plans are to connect all three trail segments to the Ohio to Erie Trail north of Dresden.

PARKING:

Trail users can park at the lot next to the trail access at Market Street in downtown Zanesville. Parking is also available along the bikeway in Riverview Park along the Muskingum River and on Main Street south of Dresden.

FOR MORE INFORMATION:

Muskingum Recreational Trail:
Muskingum Recreational Trail
P.O. Box 3042, Zanesville, OH 43702
740-455-8531

Zanes Landing Trail:
City of Zanesville
401 Market St., Zanesville, OH 43701
740-455-0609

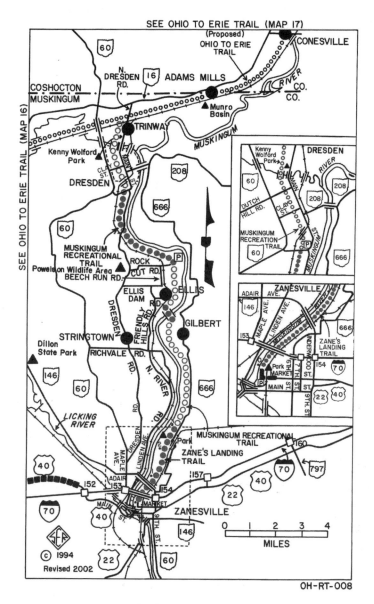

OH-RT-008

MUSKINGUM RECREATIONAL TRAIL
MUSKINGUM COUNTY
4.5 & 0.5 MILES; SURFACE: ASPHALT

ZANE'S LANDING TRAIL
3.0 MILES; SURFACE: ASPHALT

KOKOSING GAP TRAIL

VICINITY: *Mt. Vernon*
TRAIL LENGTH: *13.2 Miles*
SURFACE: *Asphalt*
TRAIL USE:

MOCHICAN VALLEY TRAIL

VICINITY: *Danville*
TRAIL LENGTH: *4.6 Miles*
SURFACE: *Smooth Crushed Gravel*
TRAIL USE:

Both the Kokosing Gap Trail and the Mohican Valley Trail were converted from the same Pennsylvania Railroad grade.

The Kokosing Gap Trail opened in 1991. The trail crosses the Kokosing River twice over two steel span bridges. Much of the trail runs through forested hills along the Kokosing River, while other scenery includes wetlands, family farms and villages. The trail starts in Mt. Vernon (Phillips Park) and goes east to historic Gambier, home of Kenyon College and many fine antique stores, shops and boutiques. The trail continues northeast from Gambier to Howard, passing under the US Route-36 stone Arch Tunnel. From there, the trail proceeds to Danville, where users can take advantage of the town's restaurants and shops. Trail users can go a few blocks through Danville to reach the Mohican Valley Trail. The Mohican Valley Trail opened to the public in 1999. The main attraction on this trail is the "Bridge of Dreams," a covered bridge built on top of a high trestle over the Mohican River.

PARKING:
Parking can be found for both trails in Mt. Vernon, Gambier, Howard, Danville and along the road under the "Bridge of Dreams."

A stone arch under US-Route-36 in Howard.

FOR MORE INFORMATION:

Kokosing Gap Trail
P.O. Box 129, Gambier, OH 43022
740-427-4509 or 740-587-6267

Mohican Valley Trail Board
P.O. Box 90, Danville,OH 43014
740-599-7900

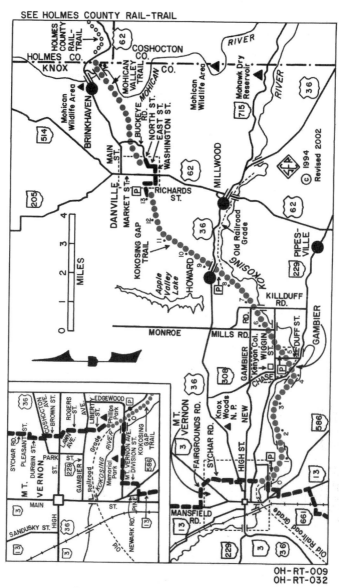

OH-RT-009
OH-RT-032

KOKOSING GAP TRAIL
KNOX COUNTY
13.2 MILES; SURFACE: ASPHALT
MOHICAN VALLEY TRAIL
4.6 MILES; SURFACE: SMOOTH
CRUSHED GRAVEL

MAD RIVER BIKEWAY (BIKE ROUTE-8)

VICINITY: *Dayton/Fairborn*
TRAIL LENGTHS, SURFACES & USES:
(MAD RIVER BIKEWAY) *2.9 Miles; Asphalt*

(HUFFMAN PRAIRIE OVERLOOK TRAIL) *4.0 Miles; Ballast*

(KAUFFMAN AVE. BIKE PATH) *4.0 Miles; Concrete & Asphalt*

The Mad River Bikeway Corridor follows the south levee of the Mad River from the River Corridor Bikeway along the Great Miami River in Dayton to Eastwood Metropark. The scenery varies from Dayton's city skyline near Webster Street to the industral ruins near Findlay Street to the scenic views of the Mad River among the natural wooded areas near Eastwood Metropark.

From here, follow the park road to the south to catch the bike path through Dayton's east side; this trail is known as the "T-Connector." From the "T-Connector," another trail goes east to Xenia. In Dayton, this trail is known as the Creekside Trail. In Greene County, this trail is known as both Bike Route-2 and the Creekside Trail which goes to the center of Xenia's hub.

Plans are being made to extend the Mad River Bikeway east from Eastwood Metropark to the Wright Brothers Memorial where two other trails start.

Senior citizens enjoy an evening stroll along the Mad River Bikeway.

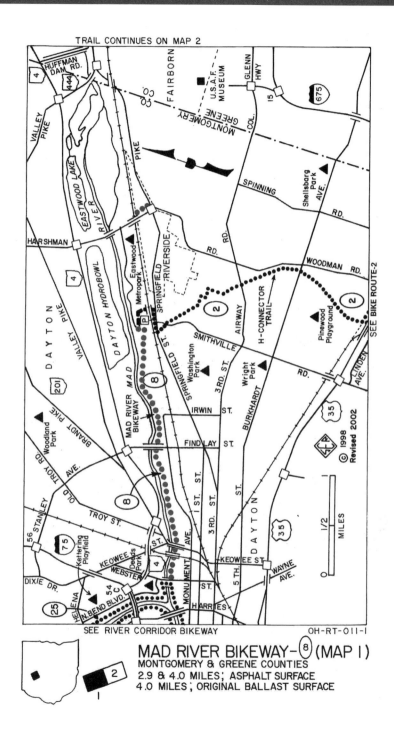

TRAIL CONTINUES ON MAP 2

HUFFMAN DAM RD.

FAIRBORN

U.S.A.F. MUSEUM

GLENN HWY

675

VALLEY PIKE

EASTWOOD LAKE

RIVER

MONTGOMERY CO. GREENE CO. COL.

15

SPINNING

Shellsborg Park AVE.

HARSHMAN

Eastwood Metropark

SPRINGFIELD ST.

RIVERSIDE

RD.

WOODMAN RD.

DAYTON HYDROBOWL

VALLEY PIKE

4

DAYTON

201

MAD RIVER

MAD RIVER BIKEWAY

8

AIRWAY

H-CONNECTOR TRAIL

2

Pinewood Playground

SEE BIKE ROUTE-2

2

SMITHVILLE

Washington Park

3RD. ST.

Wright Park

BURKHARDT

RD.

LINDEN AVE.

IRWIN ST.

FINDLAY ST.

35

BRANDT PIKE

Woodland Park

TROY RD OLD

AVE.

1 ST. ST.

3 RD. ST.

ST.

© 1998 Revised 2002

STANLEY

TROY ST.

8

56

75

Kettering Playfield

KEOWEE

Deeds Park

WEBSTER

4

DIXIE DR.

HELENA

54

N.BEND BLVD.

25

MONUMENT AVE.

ST.

KEOWEE ST.

5 TH. ST.

DAYTON

35

WAYNE AVE.

HARRIES

1/2

MILES

0

SEE RIVER CORRIDOR BIKEWAY

OH-RT-011-1

MAD RIVER BIKEWAY-⑧(MAP 1)
MONTGOMERY & GREENE COUNTIES
2.9 & 4.0 MILES; ASPHALT SURFACE
4.0 MILES; ORIGINAL BALLAST SURFACE

2

1

Both the Kauffman Avenue Bike Path and the Huffman Prairie Overlook Trail will be incorporated into the Mad River Bikeway. The Huffman Prairie Overlook Trail follows two different abandoned railroad grades, and parallels an active railroad. This rail-trail also parallels the Kauffman Avenue Bike Path, a 4-mile stretch of concrete and asphalt open to bicyclists and other users.

The Huffman Prairie Overlook Trail is a portion of the Buckeye Trail System taking hikers from Huffman Dam to Fairborn. The Kauffman Avenue Bike Path connects the Wright Brothers Memorial to the Wright State University and to the City of Fairborn.

PARKING:
Parking for the Mad River Bikeway can be found in Eastwood Metropark. Parking can also be found at the Wright Brothers Memorial on the west end of the Kauffman Avenue Bike Path.

Book author Shawn E. Richardson bikes the Kauffman Avenue Bike Path.

FOR MORE INFORMATION:
Miami Valley Regional Bicycle
Council, Inc.
333 W. 1st St., Suite 150
Dayton, OH 45402
937-463-2707

Miami Valley Regional Bicycle
Council, Inc.
1304 Horizon Dr., Fairborn, OH 45324
937-879-2068 or 937-255-4097

Greene County Parks
651 Dayton-Xenia Rd., Xenia, OH 45385
937-376-7440

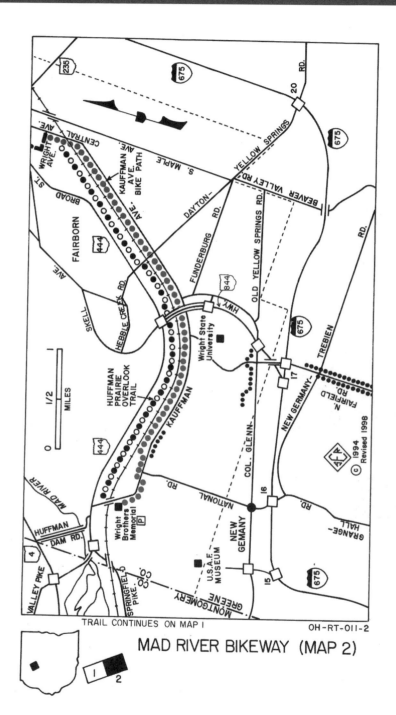

MAD RIVER BIKEWAY (MAP 2)

TRAIL CONTINUES ON MAP I

OH-RT-OII-2

23

NICKELPLATE TRAIL

VICINITY: *Louisville*
TRAIL LENGTH: *1.5 Miles*
SURFACE: *Asphalt*
TRAIL USE:

The 88 acres of Metzger Park were donated to the City of Louisville by Mary C. Metzger, whose will stated that the land should be used as a park. The 1.5 miles of asphalt paved rail-trail that forms the Nickelplate Trail runs past Metzger Park diagonally from northwest to southeast. The trail also connects with a network of smaller asphalt paths in the park creating a total of 2.5 miles.

Scenery along the Nickelplate Trail consists mostly of meadows and woods. The tranquil trail is dotted with benches for users to stop and enjoy the sounds of nature. Future plans for the park include adding recreation fields, and possibly extending the Nickelplate Trail to the southeast.

PARKING:

A parking lot located on the trail's southeast entrance next to Dellbrook Avenue provides the most convenient parking. However, a larger lot is located inside Metzger Park just off of Nickelplate Avenue south of Edmar Street.

While many trails have rest areas, this one along the Nickelplate Trail has been made more safe by leaving old railroad ties in place to serve as speed bumps.

FOR MORE INFORMATION:
Nickelplate Trail, Stark County Park District
5300 Tyner St. NW, Canton, OH 44708
330-477-3552

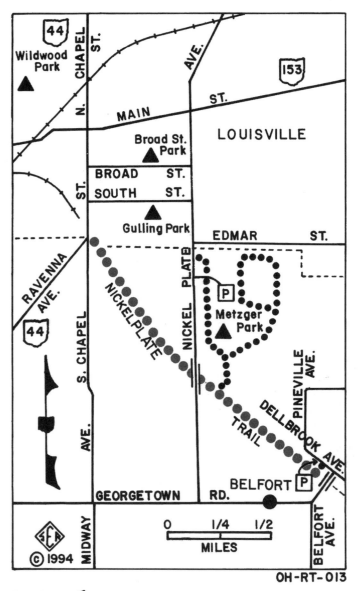

OH-RT-013

NICKELPLATE TRAIL
STARK COUNTY
1.5 MILES
SURFACE: ASPHALT

WOLF CREEK RAIL-TRAIL (BIKE ROUTE-38)

VICINITY: *Dayton*
TRAIL LENGTH: *13.0*
SURFACE: *Asphalt*
TRAIL USE: 🚴 🛼 🚶 🏕 🐎 🎿 🚶

The Wolf Creek Rail-Trail offers Dayton area residents a rural alternative to the River Corridor Bikeway. Currently 13 miles of asphalt, the trail follows the old CSX railroad grade from just west of Dayton on Olive Road and runs northwest to Verona on the Montgomery-Preble County Line.

The trail runs through a relatively flat section of Montgomery County where colorful woods, picturesque meadows and family farms make it a very scenic route. Users may wish to stop off in Trotwood to have a bite at local restaurants or visit the preserved train depot to see its display of old cabooses. Trail users can camp at Sycamore State Park, the most scenic part of the trail. Further up the trail, Brookville plays host to a second preserved depot, as well as many fine shops, restaurants and Golden Gate Park. From Brookville, the trail continues northwest under Interstate-70 through the countryside to Dodson, Bachman, Wengerlawn and Verona.

Possible future plans for the Wolf Creek Bikeway include expanding the trail in both directions. One idea extends the trail from Olive Road southeast into Dayton to connect with the James McGee Boulevard Bike Path and the River Corridor Bikeway. Another plan involves extending the trail northwest from Verona to Greenville. For current information write to the address below.

PARKING:
Parking for this trail can be found along the streets of Trotwood and Brookville.

The Trotwood Trestle over Wolf Creek (mile post 7).

FOR MORE INFORMATION:
Five Rivers Metroparks
1375 E. Siebenthaler, Dayton, OH 45414
937-275-7275

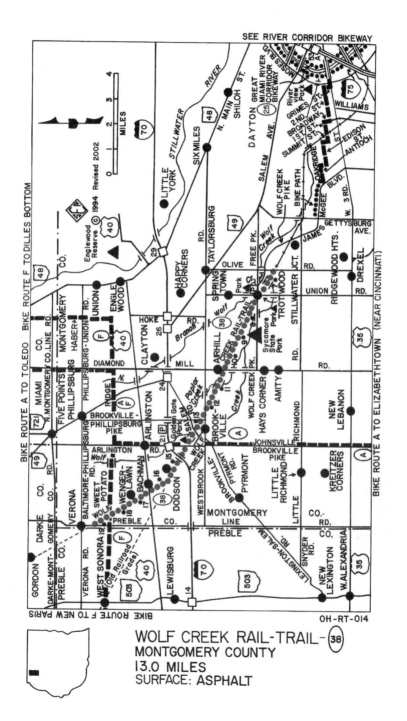

WOLF CREEK RAIL-TRAIL – (38)
MONTGOMERY COUNTY
13.0 MILES
SURFACE: ASPHALT

UNIVERSITY-PARKS HIKE-BIKE TRAIL

VICINITY: *Toledo*
TRAIL LENGTH: *6.2 Miles*
SURFACE: *Asphalt*
TRAIL USE: 🚲 🛼 🚶 🏕 🐎 🎿 ♿

Even before workers paved the University-Parks Hike-Bike Trail, mountain bicyclists and hikers in western Toledo used the path extensively. The six-mile asphalt trail starts at Toledo's west end on King Road between Central Avenue and Sylvania Avenue near Milton Olander Park, and runs east to the University of Toledo Campus.

From King Road, the trail goes east under Interstate-475 and US Route-23 before reaching Sylvania Road, where it curves and intersects with another trail leading into Wildwood Preserve Metropark. The Metropark offers users a variety of recreational activities, as well as many scenic foot paths and a loop bicycle trail. Past the Metropark, the trail crosses two bridges over Central Avenue and Secor Road on its way to the University of Toledo Campus. This section of the trail parallels an active railroad, but a thicket of trees separates the two corridors so well that users may hardly even notice the railroad.

While the rail-trail currently ends at the University of Toledo Campus, future plans include connecting it to a nearby network of bike trails that run through Ottawa Park, Jermain Park and the University of Toledo Scott Park campus. For current information contact the address below.

PARKING:
Parking for this trail can be found in Wildwood Preserve Metropark.

The University-Parks Hike-Bike Trail has a stoplight in Toledo.

FOR MORE INFORMATION:
Toledo Area Metroparks
5100 W. Central, Toledo, OH 43615
419-535-3050

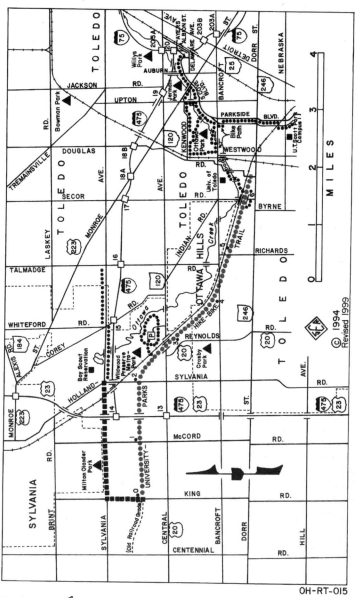

OH-RT-015

UNIVERSITY—PARKS HIKE-BIKE TRAIL
LUCAS COUNTY
6.2 MILES
TRAIL SURFACE : ASPHALT

29

GALLIPOLIS BIKE PATH

VICINITY: *Gallipolis*
TRAIL LENGTH: *3.3 and 4.5 Miles*
SURFACE: *Smooth Crushed Gravel*
TRAIL USE: 🚲 🚵 🚶 👟 🐎 ⛷ 🚶

The Gallipolis Bike Path runs through a very scenic and mountainous part of the Buckeye State. The town of Gallipolis is across the Ohio River from West Virginia. The two developed trail sections form just a small part of the planned 25-mile cross-state trail, which will eventually run from Kanauga to Gallipolis, then north to Vinton and Minerton. While most of the surrounding terrain is mountainous, the trail runs through deep cuts and high fills, making it a relatively flat and spectacular journey for cyclists and hikers. Future plans include surfacing the entire trail with asphalt.

Settled by French immigrants in 1790, Gallipolis is one of southern Ohio's most picturesque historical towns. Trail users can follow side streets seven blocks to the town's center where its main park faces the Ohio River and features a restored 1878 bandstand. Gallipolis also offers trail users several restaurants at which to stop and enjoy a meal in the east end of town.

PARKING:
Parking can be found along the streets of Gallipolis, Kerr and Bidwell.

Joyce A. Richardson pauses along the Gallipolis Bike Path.

FOR MORE INFORMATION:
Gallia County Rails-to-Trails
O.O. McIntyre Park District, 18 Locust St., Rm. 1262
Gallipolis, OH 45631
740-446-4612

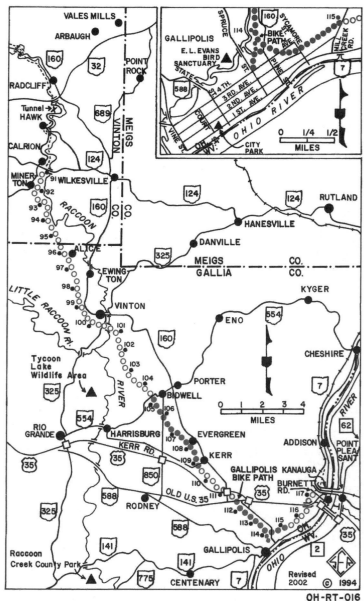

GALLIPOLIS BIKE PATH
GALLIA CO.
3.3 MILES & 4.5 MILES
SURFACE: SMOOTH CRUSHED GRAVEL

OH-RT-016

WABASH CANNONBALL TRAIL

VICINITY: *Toledo*
TRAIL LENGTH: *65.0 Miles (Trail Incomplete)*
SURFACE: *Asphalt & Smooth/Coarse Crushed Gravel*
TRAIL USE: 🚴 🛼 🚶 💺 🐎 ⛷ 🚶

MIAMI & ERIE CANAL TOWPATH TRAIL

VICINITY: *Toledo*
TRAIL LENGTH: *10.1 Miles*
SURFACE: *Mostly Dirt; sections are also Concrete, Smooth Crushed Gravel and Gravel.*
TRAIL USE: 🚴 🛼 🚶 💺 🐎 ⛷ 🚶

WABASH CANNONBALL TRAIL

Second in length only to the Little Miami Scenic Trail, the 65-mile Wabash Cannonball Trail promises to become a wonderful recreational resource to residents and visitors of Toledo and Northwestern Ohio. A great deal of development, however, still awaits the trail. So far, only 3 sections of the trail contain an asphalt surface. The first section is within the city of White House, the second section is between Monclova and the Fulton County Line, and the third section is within the city of Wauseon. Various smooth-course crushed gravel sections are open from the Lucas County Line to State Route-109, Burlington to West Unity, and Liberty (6C) to Monclova (Black Rd.).

Near future plans for the Wabash Cannonball Trail include continuing the clearing and regrading process along the undeveloped sections; some sections will also be paved. Long-range plans involve linking the trail with local bike paths in Maumee and to the North Inland Coast Bike Path, the Slippery Elm Trail and the Miami & Erie Canal Towpath Trail, providing Northwest Ohio with a major network of greenways.

The Wabash Cannonball Trail (Oak Openings Preserve).

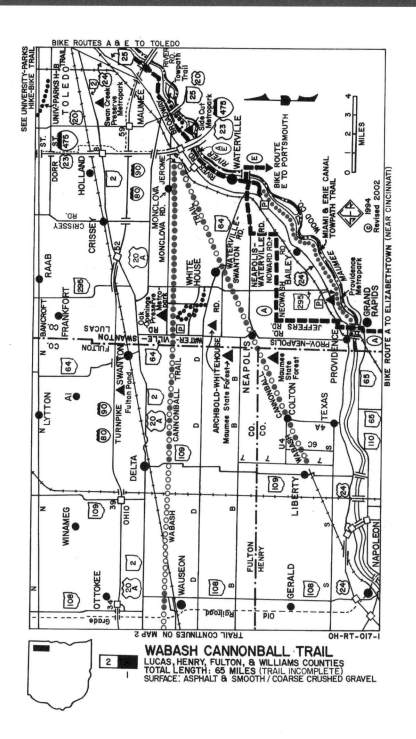

WABASH CANNONBALL TRAIL
LUCAS, HENRY, FULTON, & WILLIAMS COUNTIES
TOTAL LENGTH: 65 MILES (TRAIL INCOMPLETE)
SURFACE: ASPHALT & SMOOTH / COARSE CRUSHED GRAVEL

33

MIAMI & ERIE CANAL TOWPATH TRAIL

Most of the Miami & Erie Canal Towpath Trail runs 10.1 miles through wooded areas between the old canal bed and the Scenic Maumee River from Providence to Waterville. Trail users will enjoy stopping along the path's smooth gravel and concrete surface between the town of Providence and Providence Metropark, where they can watch mules pull a restored canal barge along the old towpath. Between Providence Metropark and Farnsworth Metropark, the trail surface shifts to a smooth-to-moderate dirt surface that is closed to all bicycles and mountain bicycles from January to March and other periods of wet weather (although this dirt section of the trail allows for standard touring bicycles, mountain bicycles provide easier navigation of its mildly bumpy spots). The remainder of the trail, from Farnsworth Metropark to the edge of Waterville, provides users with a smooth gravel and asphalt surface.

PARKING:

At this time, parking can be found for the Wabash Cannonball Trail in Oak Openings Preserve Metropark on State Route-64. Parking can be found for the Miami & Erie Canal Towpath Trail in Providence Metropark and Waterville at the intersection of US Route-24 and River Rd.

The Maumee River Parallels the 10.1-mile Miami & Erie Canal Towpath Trail.

FOR MORE INFORMATION:

Wabash Cannonball Trail
Northwestern Ohio Rails-to-Trails
Association, Inc. (NORTA,Inc.)
P.O. Box 234, Delta, OH 43515
800-951-4788 or 419-822-4788

Miami & Erie Canal Towpath Trail
Toledo Area Metroparks
5100 W. Central, Toledo, OH 43615
419-535-3050

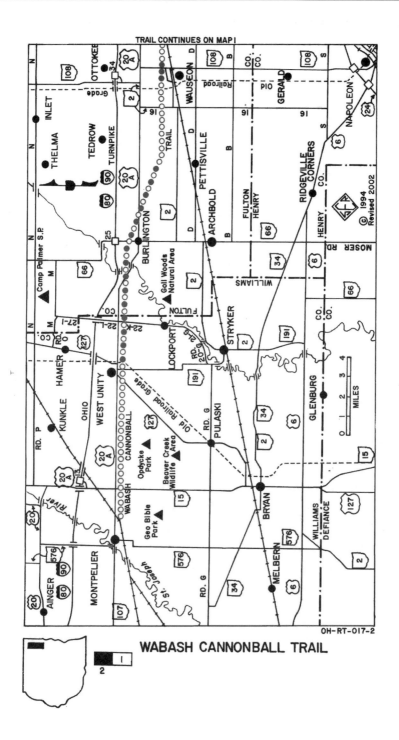

WABASH CANNONBALL TRAIL

OH-RT-017-2

NORTH COAST INLAND BIKE PATH

VICINITY: *Toledo/Elyria*
TRAIL LENGTH: *6.4 and 13.1 Miles*
SURFACE: *Asphalt*
TRAIL USE: 🚴 🚵 🚶 👟 🐎 ⛸ 🚶

The North Coast Inland Bike Path traverses across the top of Ohio roughly following US Route-20. The trail also follows the Lake Erie Coast. However, Lake Erie cannot be seen from the trail, because the route is approximately 10 miles south of the coast. This distant, parallel location explains how the North Coast Inland Bike Path received its unique name. Currently, two sections of the future 78-mile rail-trail are open; 6.4 miles in Sandusky County and 13.1 miles in Lorain County. Both trail sections consist of an asphalt surface. The trail follows the Toledo, Norwalk and Cleveland Railroad, built in 1851 connecting New York, NY to Chicago, IL. The railroad was built 10 miles away from the shore to save on the expense of building bridges and drawbridges. The railroad transported freight, produce, coal and passengers, until it was abandoned by the Penn Central Railroad in the late 1970s.

In the late 1980s, a rails-to-trails coalition was formed to convert the 78-mile railroad grade between Millbury and Elyria. In 1995, the first three miles of trail were paved through Oberlin, formerly known as the Oberlin Bike Path. In 1997, the Oberlin Bike Path was extended in both directions to Kipton and Elyria making the trail 13 miles long. During that same year, a second section was paved between Clyde and Fremont consisting of 6.4 miles.

The North Coast Inland Bike Path in Sandusky County.

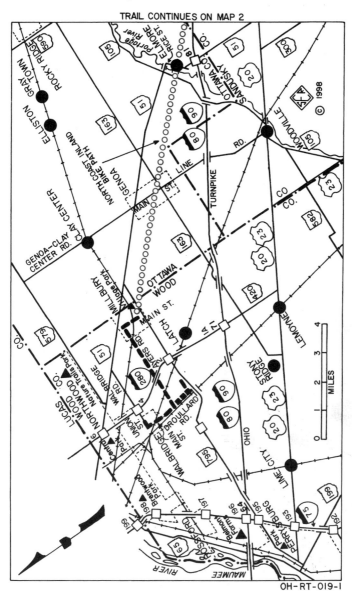

TRAIL CONTINUES ON MAP 2

OH-RT-019-1

NORTH COAST INLAND BIKE PATH (MAP I)

WOOD, OTTAWA, SANDUSKY, HURON, & LORAIN
COUNTIES: TOTAL LENGTH: 76.0 MILES
(TRAIL INCOMPLETE)
6.4 MILES; SURFACE: ASPHALT (FREMONT-CLYDE)
13.1 MILES; SURFACE: ASPHALT (KIPTON-ELYRIA)

FREMONT - CLYDE (MAPS 2 & 3)

The first stretch of rail-trail is open from Fremont to Clyde. Restaurants and lodging can be found in both Fremont and Clyde. This section parallels an existing railroad separated by woodlands and meadows. The Fremont end of the trail starts in East Side Park on St. Joseph. Between East Side Park and Smith Road, the trail parallels the north side of the railroad before switching over to the south side. Between Smith Road and the City of Clyde, the trail follows along the south side of the railroad. The terrain is mostly flat, and the scenery consists of many farms with meadows and an occasional patch of woodland. The trail ends in the center of downtown Clyde on Maple Street. Clyde is the home of the famous Sherwood Anderson, an American author.

PARKING:

Parking is available in Fremont on St. Joseph at East Side Park. Parking is also available in downtown Clyde off Maple Street.

The North Coast Inland Bike Path in Lorain County.

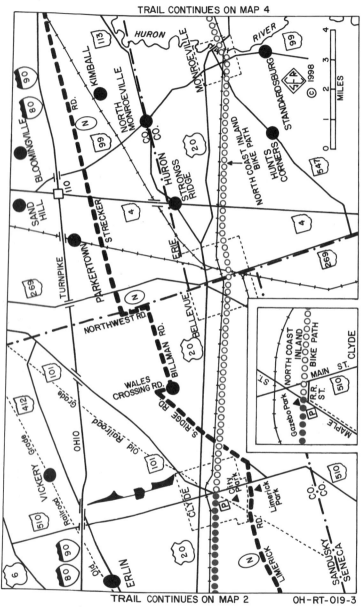

TRAIL CONTINUES ON MAP 4

NORTH COAST INLAND BIKE PATH
(MAP 3)

TRAIL CONTINUES ON MAP 2

OH-RT-019-3

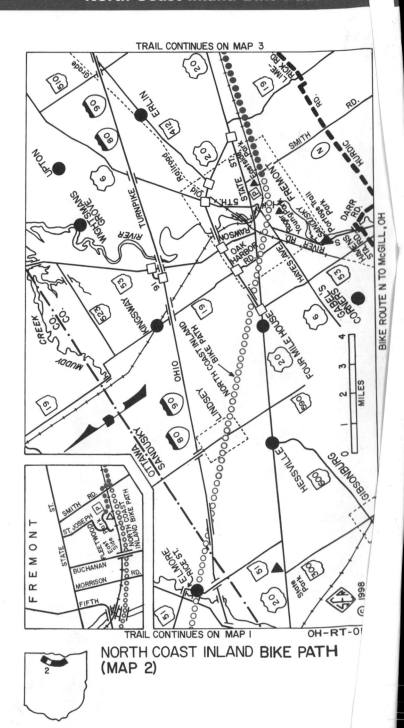

TRAIL CONTINUES ON MAP 3

BIKE ROUTE N TO McGILL, OH

MILES

NORTH COAST INLAND BIKE PATH
(MAP 2)

TRAIL CONTINUES ON MAP I

OH–RT–O

© 1998

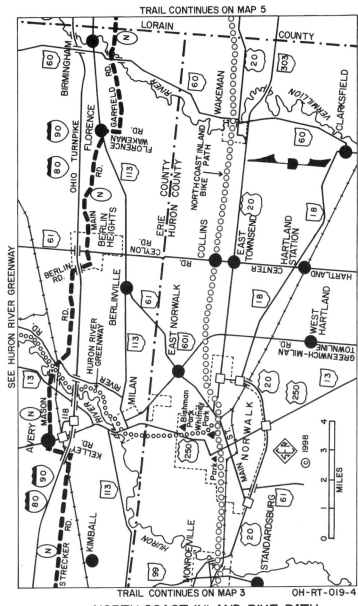

TRAIL CONTINUES ON MAP 5

TRAIL CONTINUES ON MAP 3   OH-RT-019-4

NORTH COAST INLAND **BIKE PATH**
(MAP 4)

KIPTON - ELYRIA (MAP 5)

The second stretch of rail-trail is open from Kipton through Oberlin to Elyria. Attractions along this part of the trail include Kipton Park (mile post 2), Oberlin College (mile post 7), Tappan Square (mile post 7) and the various parks in Elyria (mile post 15). The west end of the trail starts in Kipton on Baird Road (near mile post 2). From Kipton to Oberlin the terrain is also flat and the scenery consists of farms, meadows and wooded areas. The North Coast Inland Bike Path follows bike lanes along Hampton Street and Pyle-S. Amherst Road in Oberlin (between mile posts 5 and 6); lush green golf courses provide most of the scenery along this part of the trail.

In the City of Oberlin, between Pyle-S. Amherst Road and Oberlin Road (from mile posts 6 to 9), lies the original section of the former Oberlin Bike Path. Like many towns in Ohio, Oberlin shares a history of railroads that no longer exist. Oberlin, however, is more famous for a former railroad that never had a developed grade: the Underground Railroad. The Underground Railroad was the trail Harriet Tubman and other abolitionists used to help slaves escape from southern and border states to the north during the nineteenth century. Oberlin was the last stop along the Underground Railroad before fugitives slaves crossed Lake Erie into Canada. Many former slaves, however, stayed to make Oberlin their home. Today, the town's art, shops and multi-cultural events reflect its rich history of African-American culture.

Between Oberlin and Elyria (between mile posts 9 and 15), the scenery remains the same. The rail-trail ends in Elyria on Second and Third streets on the west end of town. From there, bike lanes take you along Second and Third Streets to mile post 15 in Elyria. Another scenic trail, which is not a rail-trail, follows the Black River north of Elyria. The three-mile Black River Bridgeway Trail goes through the Black River Reservation between steep bluffs. A spectacular spot is found in the middle of the trail where a zig-zag bridge had to be constructed through the deep canyon along the Black River.

PARKING:

Parking can be found in Kipton, Oberlin and Elyria.

FOR MORE INFORMATION:

Lorain County:	Sandusky County:
Lorain County Metroparks	Sandusky County Park District
12882 Diagonal Rd.	1970 Countryside Place
La Grange, OH 44050	Fremont, OH 43420
440-458-5121	419-334-4495

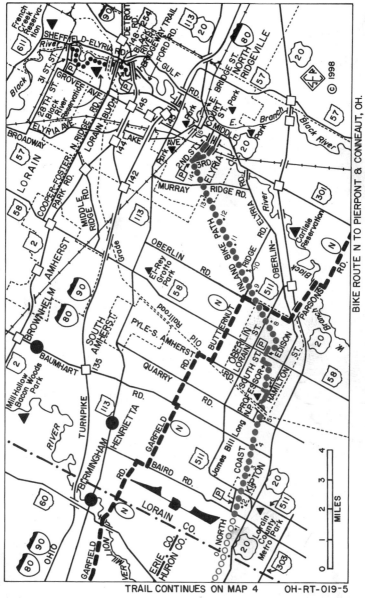

BIKE ROUTE N TO PIERPONT & CONNEAUT, OH.

© 1998

TRAIL CONTINUES ON MAP 4   OH-RT-019-5

NORTH COAST INLAND **BIKE PATH**
(MAP 5)

SLIPPERY ELM TRAIL

VICINITY: *Bowling Green*
TRAIL LENGTH: *12.0 Miles*
SURFACE: *Asphalt with paralleling Dirt*
TRAIL USE:

The Slippery Elm Trail takes its name from the trees used to build a railroad from Tontogany to Bowling Green in 1874. The original train rails were constructed by applying a thin steel plate on top of elmwood rails. The railroad was extended another 12 miles south to North Baltimore in 1890 and transported coal, freight, lumber and passengers until the 1960s. It was abandoned in 1978.

Today, a twelve-foot wide asphalt trail with a paralleling bridal path runs from North Baltimore (mile post 0/12) through Rudolph (mile post 8/4) to Bowling Green (mile post 12/0). Users enjoy relatively flat terrain along the trail's 12 miles. While part of the path passes through the last remainder of the Great Black Swamp (mile post 9/3), most of its scenery consists of farmland, green meadows and wooded areas. Trail users can find restaurants in both North Baltimore and Bowling Green.

Long-range plans could link the Slippery Elm Trail to the Miami & Erie Canal Towpath Trail, the Wabash Cannonball Trail and the North Coast Inland Bike Path to provide Northwest Ohio with a major network of greenways.

PARKING:

Parking for the Slippery Elm Trail can be found directly on each end of the trail in both North Baltimore and Bowling Green.

Horseback riders enjoy the Slippery Elm Trail.

FOR MORE INFORMATION:

Wood County Park District
18729 Mercer Rd., Bowling Green, OH 43402
419-353-1897

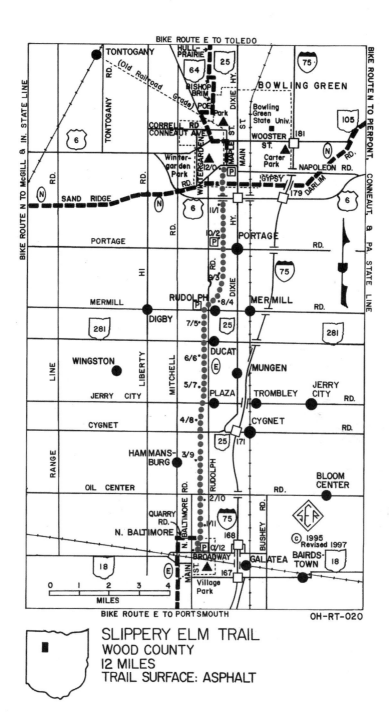

SLIPPERY ELM TRAIL
WOOD COUNTY
12 MILES
TRAIL SURFACE: ASPHALT

45

RICHLAND B. & O. TRAIL

VICINITY: *Mansfield*
TRAIL LENGTH: *18.3 Miles*
SURFACE: *Asphalt*
TRAIL USE: 🚲 🛼 🚶 ♿ 🐎 ⛷ 🚶

The Richland B. & O. Trail runs from Butler to Mansfield to form a crescent in the southern part of Richland County. This rail-trail follows the former Baltimore & Ohio Railroad through the towns of Butler, Bellville, Lexington and Mansfield, and its scenery includes picturesque farmland and rolling hills.

The trail begins in Butler (mile post 0), home of the Clear Fork Ski Area and just four miles southwest of Malabar Farm State Park, famous for its home-made maple syrup. The path follows the Clear Fork Mohican River from Butler to Lexington, passing through Bellville (mile post 5) and crossing the river five times. In Lexington (mile post 11), where the trail leaves the banks of the Clear Fork Mohican, users can stop to visit the Gorman Nature Center Park and Richland County Historical Society. The trail goes north from Lexington through Alta (mile post 15), to enter Mansfield from its west side before ending next to North Lake Park (mile post 18). A bridge guides trail users between the bike path and the park. For further information on the Richland B. & O. Trail, contact the addresses below.

PARKING:
Parking for this trail can be found in Butler, Bellville, Lexington, Alta and in North Lake Park on Rowland Street in Mansfield.

A cyclist enjoys the beautiful countryside along the Richland B. & O. Trail.

FOR MORE INFORMATION:

Mansfield-Richland Visitors Bureau
52 Park Ave. West
Mansfield, OH 44902
419-525-1300

Richland County Park District
2295 Lexington Ave.
Mansfield, OH 44907
419-884-3764

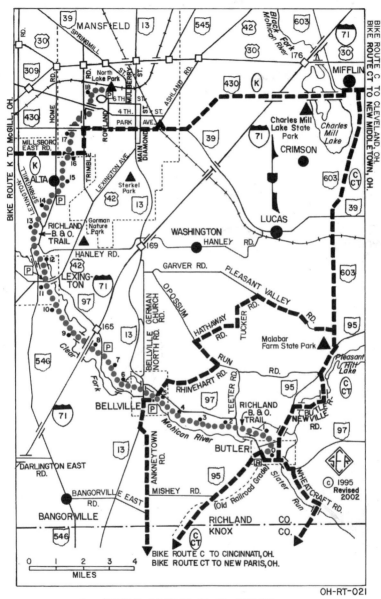

OH-RT-021

RICHLAND B. & O. TRAIL
RICHLAND CO.
18 MILES
SURFACE : ASPHALT

BIKE ROUTE-3 (XENIA-JAMESTOWN TRAIL)

VICINITY: *Xenia*
TRAIL LENGTH: *1.2 Miles (Will be 11.0 Miles)*
SURFACE: *Asphalt*
TRAIL USE:

Bike Route-3 is also known as the Xenia-Jamestown Trail (to open in 2006). The trail roughly parallels US Route-35. The trail starts in Xenia at the Xenia Station, a historical replica of the original Xenia Hub Station, where the trains on the railroads converged from five different directions. Today, the trail users converge on the bike paths from five different directions.

When Bike Route-3 opens, it will go from Xenia in a southeast direction to New Jasper and Jamestown; this section is expected to open in 2006. Near New Jasper is Caesar's Ford Area Park and the Blue Jacket Outdoor Drama Theater, just south from the trail on New Jasper Station Road. From here, the trail goes east towards Seaman Park near Quarry Road and Cottonville Road. A trail spur connects Seaman Park to Bike Route-3, giving trail users a safe access.

Currently, Bike Route-3 is complete as an asphalt trail from Seaman Park to the center of Jamestown (State Route-72). This section of the 1.2-mile trail, formerly known as the Jamestown Bikeway, was opened during the mid 1990s as a gravel trail, giving the citizens of Jamestown a safe access to the ballfields in Seaman Park. Immediately, the trail became so popular that it was given an asphalt trail surface by 1998.

When complete, Bike Route-3 will traverse 12 miles through southeastern Greene County from Xenia to Jamestown. An extension is planned for Bike Route-3 to go east from Jamestown to Washington, C.H.; this would give trail users a direct connection to the Tri-County Triangle Trail.

PARKING:
Parking is available at the Xenia Hub Station in the center of Xenia, and in Seaman Park off of Cottonville Road in Jamestown.

FOR MORE INFORMATION:
Greene County Parks
651 Dayton-Xenia Rd., Xenia, OH 45385
937-562-7440 or 937-562-7445

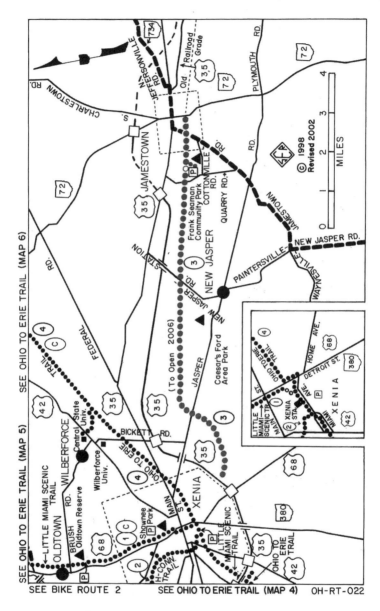

BIKE ROUTE 3
GREENE COUNTY
1.2 MILES (WILL BE 12.0 MILES)
SURFACE: ASPHALT

HOCKHOCKING-ADENA BIKEWAY
VICINITY: *Athens*
TRAIL LENGTH: *11.5 Miles*
SURFACE: *Asphalt*
TRAIL USE:

RIVERSIDE BIKEWAY
VICINITY: *Athens*
TRAIL LENGTH: *5.0 Miles*
SURFACE: *Asphalt*
TRAIL USE:

The 16.5-mile Hockhocking-Adena Bikeway is located in the Appalachian area of southeastern Ohio between Athens and Nelsonville. The Bikeway is named after the first inhabitants of this region. "Hockhocking," meaning "twisted," was the Native American Indian name of the Hocking River. Adena is a reflection of the history of the Adena Indians, who lived in this valley more than 2000 years ago. Originally constructed between 1829 and 1842, the Hocking Canal connected the Ohio River with the popular Ohio to Erie Canal. In 1870, the towpath was replaced by the Old Columbus and Hocking Valley Railroad. By 1996, the railway became a bikeway.

The trail starts on the east side of Athens along East State Street just east of US Route-33 (mile post 0). Between mile posts 0 and 5, the trail follows the Hocking River around the Ohio University Campus; this section is not a rail-trail. Between mile posts 5 and 16.5, the trail follows the railroad grade. Attractions along the trail include Wayne National Forest (between mile post 12 and 14) and the Hocking College Campus in Nelsonville (mile post 16.5).

PARKING:
Parking can be found in Athens, The Plains and Nelsonville.

The Hockhocking-Adena Bikeway trestle near mile post 5.

FOR MORE INFORMATION:
Athens County Convention and Visitors Bureau
607 E. State St., Athens, OH 45701
800-878-9767

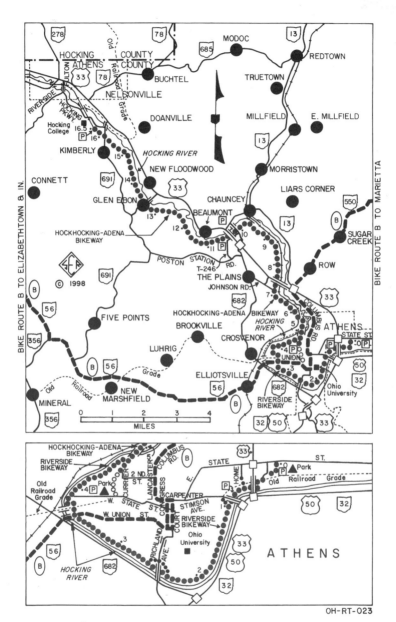

OH-RT-023

HOCKHOCKING-ADENA/RIVERSIDE BIKEWAYS
ATHENS COUNTY
16.5 MILES
SURFACE: ASPHALT

BIKE ROUTE-2 (DAYTON-XENIA TRAIL)

VICINITY: *Dayton/Xenia*
TRAIL LENGTH: *15.9 Miles*
SURFACE: *Asphalt*
TRAIL USE:

Bike Route-2, also known as the Creekside Trail, was formerly known as the H-Connector Trail. The trail roughly parallels US Route-35. The trail starts in Xenia at the Xenia Station, a historical replica of the original Xenia Hub Station, where the trains on the railroads converged from five different directions (mile post 0). Today, the trail users converge on the bike paths from five different directions.

The trail goes northwest from Xenia to Trebein (mile post 4), Alpha (mile post 6), Beaver Creek (between mile posts 6 and 11) and Dayton. Attractions along Bike Route-2 in Greene County are Solarnovitz Park, James Ranch West Side Park and the Greene County Fairgrounds in Xenia (mile post 1). Other attractions include the Glenn Thompson Reserve next to the Little Miami River (between mile posts 4 and 5), Alpha Mill (mile post 6), Beaver Creek Community Park (mile post 6), Nutter Park (mile post 7) and 5/3 Gateway Park (mile post 10). A view of the Interstate-675 and US Route-35 interchange can be seen from a spectacularly converted railroad bridge over Interstate-675 (mile post 10).

The attractions along the trail in Montgomery County and the City of Dayton are Pinewood Park, Eastwood Metropark and the Mad River. Near Pinewood Park, the bike path has a spur to the south, passing under US Route-35 to reach Linden and Woodbine Avenues. In Eastwood Metropark, this bike path connects to the Mad River Bikeway. Following the Mad River Bikeway along Mad River in a southwest direction will bring you to downtown Dayton and the River Corridor Bikeway.

PARKING:
Parking is available at the Xenia Hub Station in the Center of Xenia, Factory Road in Beaver Creek, Dayton-Xenia Road near Interstate-675 and Eastwood Metropark in Dayton.

FOR MORE INFORMATION:
Greene County Parks
651 Dayton-Xenia Rd., Xenia, OH 45385
937-376-7440

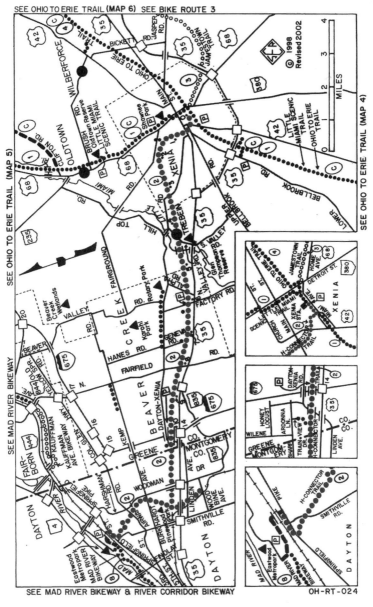

BIKE ROUTE 2
MONTGOMERY & GREENE COUNTIES
15.9 MILES
SURFACE: ASPHALT

OH-RT-024

OHIO TO ERIE TRAIL

VICINITY: *Cincinnati/Xenia/Columbus/Newark/Akron/Cleveland*
TRAIL LENGTH: *335.0 Miles (Trail Incomplete)*
SURFACE: *Asphalt, Asphalt with Dirt, and Smooth Crushed Gravel*
TRAIL USE: 🚴 🚵 🚶 🛼 🎿 🚶   (🏇 *along the Little Miami Scenic Trail*)

The Ohio to Erie Trail gets its name from its two end points, the Ohio River in Cincinnati and Lake Erie in Cleveland. The concept of this trail is to connect both existing and planned trails between the Cities of Cincinnati, Columbus and Cleveland. When complete, the Ohio to Erie Trail will be over 300 miles long and have a combination trail surface of both asphalt and smooth crushed gravel. This trail follows a combination of former railroads, former canals, river corridors and other various corridors. This trail promises to become a major attraction for recreationalists. Currently, about 181 miles of the Ohio to Erie Trail is open across the state.

TRAIL NAME	TRAIL SECTION COMPLETED	LENGTH
Lunken Airport Bike Path	Cincinnati (Eastern)	5.0 miles
Little Miami Scenic Trail / Bike Route-1	Milford-Xenia	50.0 miles
Bike Route-4	Xenia-Cedarville	18.0 miles
Heritage Rail-Trail	Plain City-Hilliard	7.5 miles
Lower Scioto / Olentangy Bikeways	Columbus (Central)	2.0 miles
Interstate-670 Bikeway	Columbus (Central-East)	3.0 miles
Evans (Thomas J.) Bike Path	Johnstown-Newark	19.0 miles
Evans (Thomas J.) Bike Path	Newark-Hanover	8.5 miles
Coshocton-Lake Park Bike Path	Coshocton	3.0 miles
Towpath Trail (Ohio, Erie Canal)	Bolivar-Massillon	15.0 miles
Towpath Trail (Ohio, Erie Canal)	Massillon-Clinton	12.0 miles
Towpath Trail (Ohio, Erie Canal)	Barberton	5.0 miles
Towpath Trail (Ohio, Erie Canal)	Downtown Akron	1.5 miles
Towpath Trail (Ohio, Erie Canal)	Akron-Cleveland	32.0 miles
OHIO TO ERIE TRAIL	TOTAL LENGTH COMPLETED:	181.5 miles

Other sections of the Ohio to Erie Trail will open within the coming years. Plans are to have most of this 335-mile cross-state trail open by 2008.

PARKING:
Parking can be found in many places along the Ohio to Erie Trail. Check each section for exact parking information.

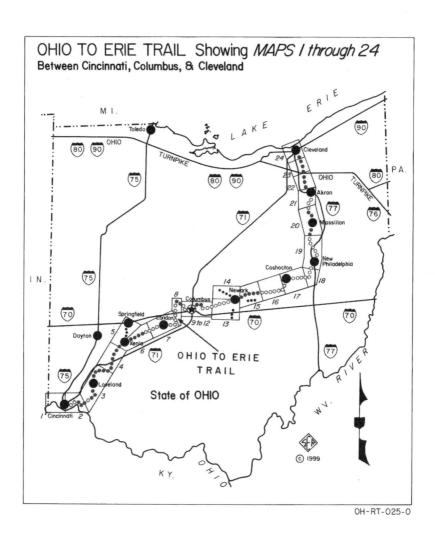

OHIO TO ERIE TRAIL Showing *MAPS 1 through 24*
Between Cincinnati, Columbus, & Cleveland

OH-RT-025-0

FOR MORE INFORMATION:
Ohio to Erie Trail Fund
P.O. Box 21246, Columbus, OH 43221
614-402-5078

A nonprofit organization can be contacted to receive the latest news and information on the developments of this very popular and growing trail.

CINCINNATI SECTION (MAPS 1 AND 2)

This section of the Ohio to Erie Trail will be known as the Cincinnati River Front Bikeway. Currently, this trail is being planned to start on the west end of Cincinnati near Anderson Ferry and will follow the Ohio River to downtown Cincinnati where the ballparks, the music and art centers, and the river boats, including the Delta Queen, can be visited. From downtown Cincinnati, the bike path will then follow the Ohio River and its spectacular high bluffs to the east along with Columbia Parkway (US Route-50) and Eastern Avenue (US Route-52) to Lunken Airport.

BIKE ROUTES B & C (MAPS 1, 2 AND 3)

Currently, two bike routes have been established to help long distance cyclists cross Cincinnati, as well as the state of Ohio. Bike Routes B & C follow a combination of back streets, back roads and even some major roads; only very experienced cyclists should use these routes during non-peak traffic hours. Until the Cincinnati River Front Bikeway is built, Bike Route-B starts on the Ohio-Indiana State Line west of Cincinnati and roughly follows the Ohio River to downtown Cincinnati, then to Lunken Airport on the east side. Bike Route-C starts in downtown Cincinnati and goes through the eastern neighborhoods of Fairfax and Mariemont to Milford where the 68-mile Little Miami Scenic Trail begins.

Cincinnati Skyline.

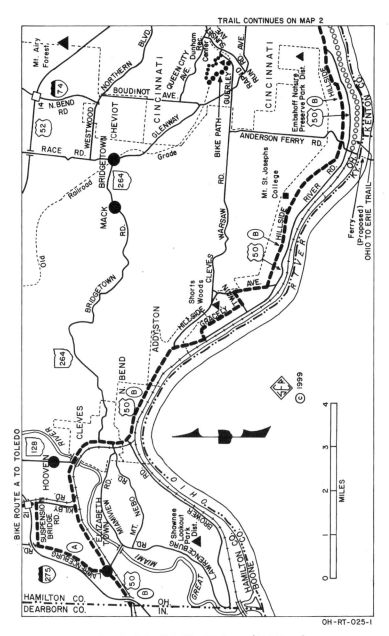

TRAIL CONTINUES ON MAP 2

OH-RT-025-1

OHIO TO ERIE TRAIL (MAP 1)
HAMILTON COUNTY
335.0 MILES (TRAIL INCOMPLETE)
SURFACE: ASPHALT

LUNKEN AIRPORT BIKE PATH *(MAP 2)*

VICINITY: *Cincinnati*
TRAIL LENGTH: *5.0 Miles*
SURFACE: *Asphalt*
TRAIL USE: 🚴 🛼 🚶 🚉 🐎 ⛷ ♿

Before the concept of the Ohio to Erie Trail was ever imagined, a circular trail was constructed during the 1970s around the Lunken Airport for nearby residents to walk, jog and bike. A facility along the Lunken Airport Bike Path includes a children's playground with a real train and airplane to play in. This bike path also goes around a local golf course. At one time, Lunken Airport was Cincinnati's main airport for larger airplanes, before it was relocated across the Ohio River in Kentucky. However, the airport itself can be considered as an attraction for trail users to see many different types of airplanes take off and land. The most scenic part of the bike path is along the southern side of the airport, especially the part that follows the Little Miami River where nature is abundant.

PARKING:
Parking is located in the local park on Wilmer Avenue right next to Beechmont Avenue (State Route-561).

Walkers and cyclists enjoy the Lunken Airport Bike Path.

CINCINNATI-MILFORD (MAPS 2 AND 3)
A proposal is being developed to connect the Lunken Airport Bike Path in Cincinnati to the Little Miami Scenic Trail in Milford. The trail will follow a combination of both sides of the Little Miami River between these two points.

FOR MORE INFORMATION:
Lunken County Airport
621 E. Mehring Way, Suite 301
Cincinnati, OH 45202
No Phone #

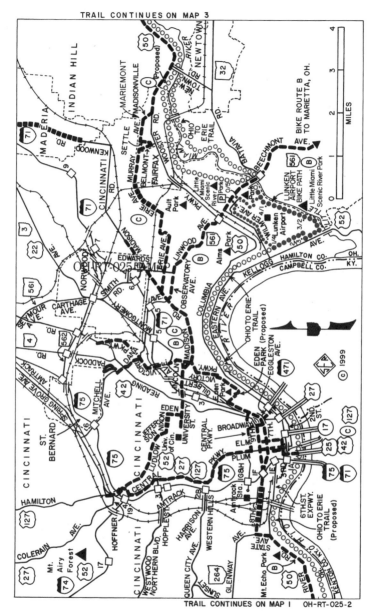

TRAIL CONTINUES ON MAP 3

BIKE ROUTE B TO MARIETTA, OH.

TRAIL CONTINUES ON MAP 1   OH-RT-025-2

OHIO TO ERIE TRAIL (MAP 2)
HAMILTON COUNTY
335.0 MILES (TRAIL INCOMPLETE)
SURFACE: ASPHALT
LUNKEN AIRPORT BIKE PATH
5.0 MILES; SURFACE: ASPHALT

MILFORD-XENIA-SPRINGFIELD SECTION (MAPS 3, 4 AND 5)
LITTLE MIAMI SCENIC TRAIL/BIKE ROUTE-1

VICINITY: *Cincinnati/Xenia/Springfield*
TRAIL LENGTH: *68.0 Miles*
SURFACE: *Asphalt with parallel Dirt*
TRAIL USE:

The most popular section of the Ohio to Erie Trail in southwestern Ohio is the Little Miami Scenic Trail. With 68 miles winding along the Little Miami River and across the region, the Little Miami Scenic Trail is the longest developed rail-trail in the Buckeye State. This trail is also known as Bike Route-1 through Greene and Clark Counties. Bike Route-C also follows the trail from Milford to Xenia. The trail starts from its south end in Milford and goes through Miamiville, Loveland, South Lebanon, Morrow, Fort Ancient State Park, Oregonia, Corwin, Waynesville, Spring Valley, Xenia, Yellow Springs and Beatty before reaching its north end in Springfield.

The trail follows the meandering Little Miami River through Hamilton, Clermont, Warren and Southern Greene Counties, offering users views of rolling farm country, small cliffs and steep gorges with outcropping rocks. Other sights include a deep forested valley with steep hillsides, several with high bridges crossing the valley. The Little Miami River Valley is rich with the history and burial grounds of Native Americans. Battles of the Revolutionary War and the French and Indian Wars were also fought here. During the first and second world wars, the railroad line that the trail now follows once helped transport ammunition manufactured at the Peters' Cartridge Company in Kings Mills.

A shady stretch of the Little Miami Scenic Trail between Loveland and Morrow.

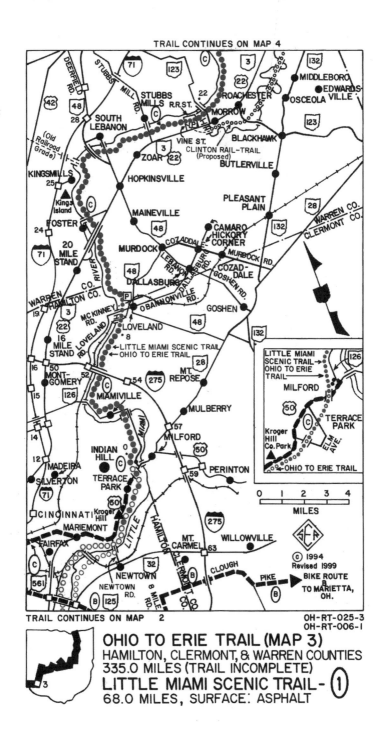

TRAIL CONTINUES ON MAP 4

TRAIL CONTINUES ON MAP 2

OH-RT-025-3
OH-RT-006-1

OHIO TO ERIE TRAIL (MAP 3)
HAMILTON, CLERMONT, & WARREN COUNTIES
335.0 MILES (TRAIL INCOMPLETE)
LITTLE MIAMI SCENIC TRAIL- ①
68.0 MILES, SURFACE: ASPHALT

As the trail goes through most of Greene and Clark Counties, it leaves the banks of the Little Miami to run through the towns of Spring Valley, Xenia, Yellow Springs, Beatty and Springfield, utilizing a steel bridge to span the river between Xenia and Yellow Springs. While much of the scenery consists of farmlands and green shady woods, this section of the trail offers highlights such as the Xenia Station in Xenia, a historical replica of the original Xenia Hub Station, where the trains on the railroads converged from five different directions. Today the trail users converge on the bike paths from five different directions. Bike Route-1 takes you north to Springfield and south to Milford. Bike Route-2 takes you west to Dayton, Bike Route-3 takes you east to Jamestown (to open in 2006), and Bike Route-4 takes you northeast to South Charleston; all of these trails are on asphalt rail-trails with no motorized vehicles. Other trail highlights include the Greene county Court House, Shawnee Park, John Bryan State Park, Glen Helen Nature Preserve, Antioch College and downtown Springfield.

Horseback riders can enjoy the dirt path paralleling the asphalt trail.

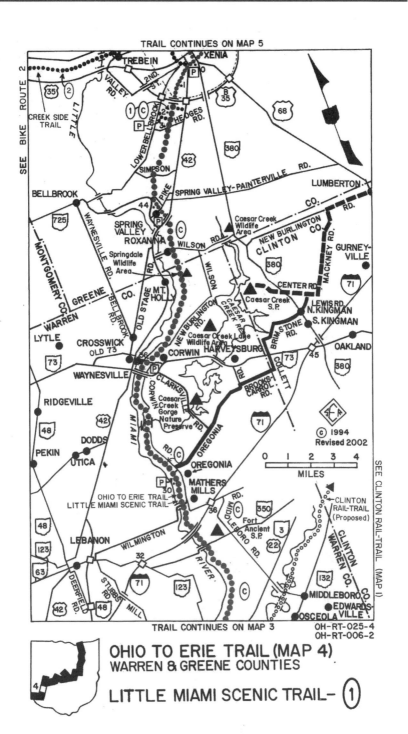

TRAIL CONTINUES ON MAP 5

OHIO TO ERIE TRAIL (MAP 4)
WARREN & GREENE COUNTIES

LITTLE MIAMI SCENIC TRAIL— ①

All trails come together in Xenia at the Xenia Station Hub.

The Little Miami Scenic trail will be extended on both ends to connect with Cincinnati's River Front Bikeway and Springfield's Buck Creek Bike Path. For current information, contact the addresses below.

PARKING:

Parking can be found in Milford, Miamiville, Loveland, Morrow, Oregonia, Corwin, Spring Valley, Xenia, Yellow Springs, Emery Chapel and along streets in Springfield.

FOR MORE INFORMATION:

State Park Section:
(Southern)

Little Miami State Park
8570 E. S.R.-73, Waynesville, OH 45068
513-897-3055

Clark County Section:
(Northern)

Springfield Parks and Recreation, City Hall
76 E. High St., Springfield, OH 45502
937-324-7348

Greene County Section:
(Central)

Greene County Parks
651 Dayton-Xenia Rd., Xenia, OH 45385
937-376-7440

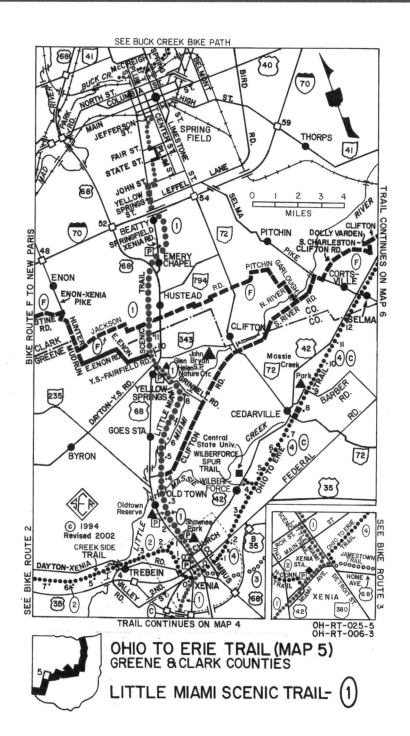

OHIO TO ERIE TRAIL (MAP 5)
GREENE & CLARK COUNTIES

LITTLE MIAMI SCENIC TRAIL— ①

XENIA-CEDARVILLE SECTION (MAP 6)
BIKE ROUTE-4 (Xenia-South Charleston Trail)
VICINITY: *Xenia*
TRAIL LENGTH: *18.0 Miles*
SURFACE: *Asphalt*
TRAIL USE: 🚴 🚵 🚶 🛼 🐎 ⛷ 🥾

WILBERFORCE SPUR TRAIL
VICINITY: *Xenia*
TRAIL LENGTH: *0.8 Miles*
SURFACE: *Asphalt*
TRAIL USE: 🚴 🚵 🚶 🛼 🐎 ⛷ 🥾

Bike Route-4 is part of the Ohio to Erie Trail from Xenia to South Charleston. The bike path roughly parallels US Route-42. The trail starts in Xenia at the Xenia Station, a historical replica of the original Xenia Hub Station where the trains on the railroads converged from five different directions (mile post 0). Today, the trail users converge on the bike paths from five different directions. Near Wilberforce-Switch Road is the Wilberforce Spur Trail which connects Bike Route-4 to Central State, Wilberforce University and the National Afro-American Museum (between mile posts 4 and 5). In Cedarville, Bike Route-4 connects to Massie Creek Park (mile post 8) before reaching Barber Road (mile post 8.7). Cyclists will notice the gradual uphill grade from Xenia to South Charleston; the scenery consists mostly of open farmland and some wooded spots. Future plans are to extend Bike Route-4 northeast to London.

PARKING:
Parking can be found in Xenia at the Xenia Station and Cedarville in Massie Creek Park.

CEDARVILLE-PLAIN CITY SECTION (MAPS 6, 7 AND 8)
Currently, plans are to follow the old railroad grade from Cedarville (map 6), to Georgesville (map 7) passing through the cities of South Charleston, London and Lilly Chapel. From there, the Ohio to Erie Trail will follow Darby Creek from Georgesville to West Jefferson and Plain City (map 8). The Heritage Rail-Trail goes from Plain City to Hilliard (map 8), just outside of Columbus.

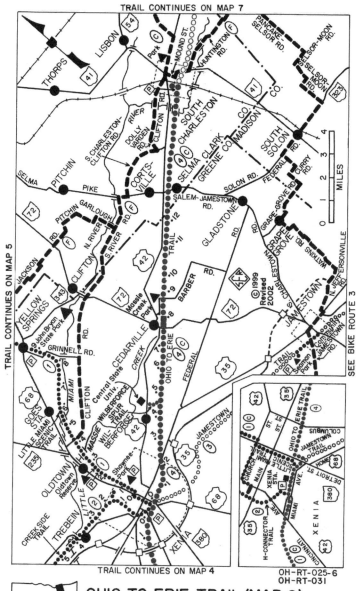

TRAIL CONTINUES ON MAP 7

TRAIL CONTINUES ON MAP 4

OH-RT-025-6
OH-RT-031

OHIO TO ERIE TRAIL (MAP 6)
GREENE & CLARK COUNTIES
335.0 MILES (TRAIL INCOMPLETE)
SURFACE: ASPHALT
BIKE ROUTE 4 PRAIRIE PATH
18.0 MILES ; SURFACE: ASPHALT
WILBERFORCE SPUR TRAIL
GREENE CO.; 0.8 MILES ; SURFACE: ASPHALT

BIKE ROUTE-C (SEE MAPS 6, 7 AND 8)

Bike Route-C has been established to help long distance cyclists cross the state of Ohio. Bike Route-C follows mostly back roads and sometimes major roads; only the very experienced cyclists should use this route. Until the Ohio to Erie Trail is built from South Charleston to Plain City, Bike Route-C can be traveled from South Charleston to Plain City (42 miles). Bike Route-C can be reached from South Charleston by taking State Route-41 to US Route-42 which Bike Route-C follows (see map 6). This route goes through Clark and Madison Counties between the two cities. The back roads in this part of Ohio vary from gently rolling to flat. The scenery consists mostly of rural farmland. Bike Route-C goes just east of Plain City on Cemetery Pike where the Heritage Rail-Trail begins.

A rural farm between Xenia and London on the Ohio to Erie Trail.

FOR MORE INFORMATION:
Greene County Parks
651 Dayton-Xenia Rd., Xenia, OH 45385
937-376-7440

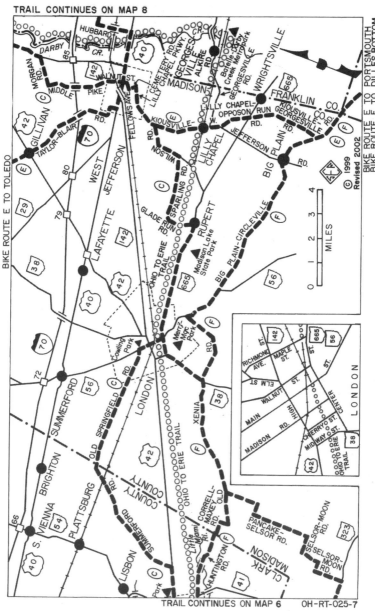

TRAIL CONTINUES ON MAP 8

TRAIL CONTINUES ON MAP 6

OH-RT-025-7

OHIO TO ERIE TRAIL (MAP 7)
CLARK, MADISON, & FRANKLIN COUNTIES

PLAIN CITY TO HILLIARD SECTION (MAP 8)
HERITAGE RAIL-TRAIL

VICINITY: *Columbus*
TRAIL LENGTH: *7.5 Miles (Trail Incomplete)*
SURFACE: *Asphalt*
TRAIL USE: 🚲 🚵 🕴 🎿 🚶 (🐎 *between Cemetery Pike & Hayden Run Rd.*)

The Heritage Rail-Trail provides users in the Northwest area of Columbus and Franklin County with a great recreational opportunity. The trail goes from Plain City to Hilliard. Plain City has a very small Amish community and two fine Amish restaurants on US Route-42. The center of Hilliard on Main Street is known as "Old Hilliard" with historical buildings, brick sidewalks and old-fashioned street lamps lining Main Street.

From Cemetery Pike in Plain City, the rail-trail goes southeast to Hayden Run Road in Hilliard. A new metropark is adjacent to this section of the trail. From Hayden Run Road, the rail-trail passes by Homestead Park, which offers users a variety of recreational facilities including shelter for outings, elaborate playgrounds and a circular recreational trail adjacent to the Heritage Rail- Trail. From here, the trail continues southeast to the center of Old Hilliard on Main Street, where the trail currently ends and/or begins. Future plans are to extend the Heritage Rail-Trail southeast to the Scioto River in Columbus.

PARKING:
Parking is available in the center of Old Hilliard and at Homestead Park on Gosgray Road.

Rob and Michael Longest bike the Heritage Rail-Trail through Old Hilliard.

FOR MORE INFORMATION:
Heritage Rail-Trail Coalition
c/o Homestead Park, 4675 Cosgray Rd., Amlin, OH 43002
614-876-9554 or 614-876-2020

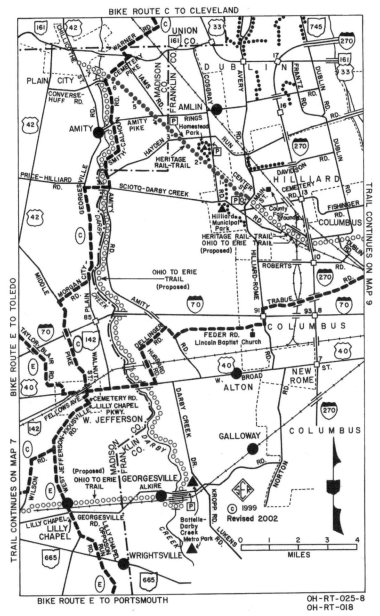

OHIO TO ERIE TRAIL (MAP 8)
MADISON & FRANKLIN COUNTIES
335.0 MILES (TRAIL INCOMPLETE)
HERITAGE RAIL-TRAIL
7.5 MILES (TRAIL INCOMPLETE)
SURFACE: ASPHALT

OH-RT-025-8
OH-RT-018

HILLIARD-COLUMBUS SECTION (MAPS 8, 9 AND 10)

A long-range plan is in the works to extend the Heritage Rail-Trail from Hilliard southeast to the Scioto River; this portion will parallel both the existing railroad and Scioto-Darby Road. Another trail is being planed along the Upper Scioto River through Columbus from Upper Arlington to downtown Columbus. The Lower Scioto Bikeway can be taken from Grandview Avenue to downtown Columbus. Unfortunately, there are not any good back roads for cyclists to follow from Hilliard to Columbus. However, certain back streets can be taken through downtown Columbus to reach the Interstate-670 Bikeway.

Ohio's State Capitol is just a few blocks from the Ohio to Erie Trail in downtown Columbus.

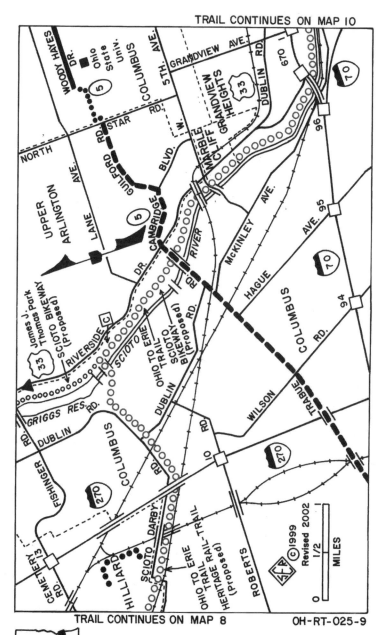

TRAIL CONTINUES ON MAP 10

TRAIL CONTINUES ON MAP 8

OH-RT-025-9

OHIO TO ERIE TRAIL (MAP 9)
FRANKLIN COUNTY; 335.0 MILES (INCOMPLETE)

COLUMBUS SECTION (MAPS 10 AND 11)
INTERSTATE-670 BIKEWAY

VICINITY: *Columbus*
TRAIL LENGTH: *3.0 Miles*
SURFACE: *Asphalt*
TRAIL USE:

Formerly a railroad yard, this area was transformed to include new streets, Interstate-670, and its own rail-trail, known as the I-670 Bikeway. Only one active Conrail line remains. Plans continue for the three-mile trail to connect with Port Columbus International, as well as to other existing trails in Columbus, including the Ohio to Erie Trail.

PARKING:
There are currently no designated parking areas for this trail.

The Skyline of Columbus is part of the Ohio to Erie Trail.

COLUMBUS-NEWARK (MAPS 11, 12 AND 13)
A long-range plan is in the works to connect Columbus's and Newark's network of bike paths. A 30-mile rail-trail will parallel an existing railroad between both cities passing through Pataskala. This will connect the I-670 Bikeway to the Evans Bike Path on James Road in the southwestern part of Newark.

FOR MORE INFORMATION:
City of Columbus, Division of Traffic Engineering
109 N. Front St., Columbus, OH 43215
614-645-7790

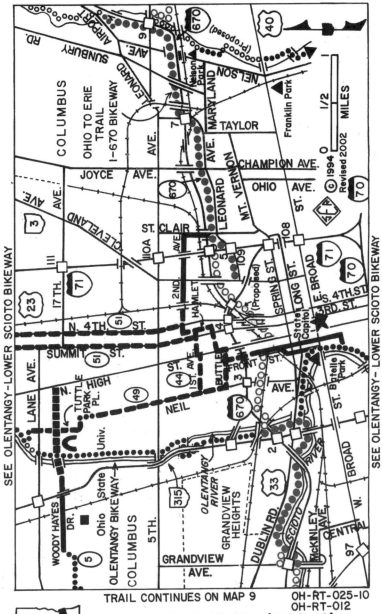

TRAIL CONTINUES ON MAP 11

TRAIL CONTINUES ON MAP 9

OH-RT-025-10
OH-RT-012

OHIO TO ERIE TRAIL (MAP 10)
FRANKLIN COUNTY; 335.0 MILES (INCOMPLETE)
I-670 BIKEWAY
3.0 MILES; SURFACE: ASPHALT

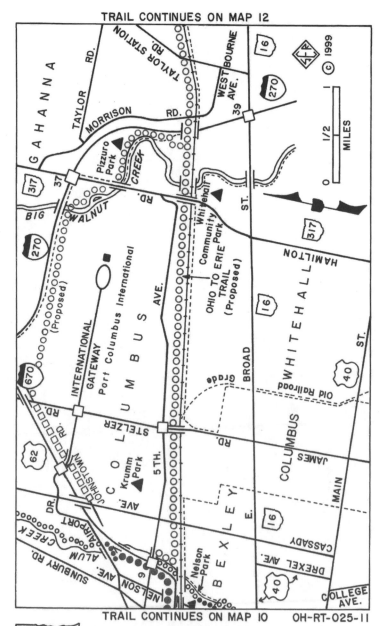

TRAIL CONTINUES ON MAP 12

TRAIL CONTINUES ON MAP 10

OH-RT-025-11

OHIO TO ERIE TRAIL (MAP 11)
FRANKLIN COUNTY; 335.0 MILES (INCOMPLETE)

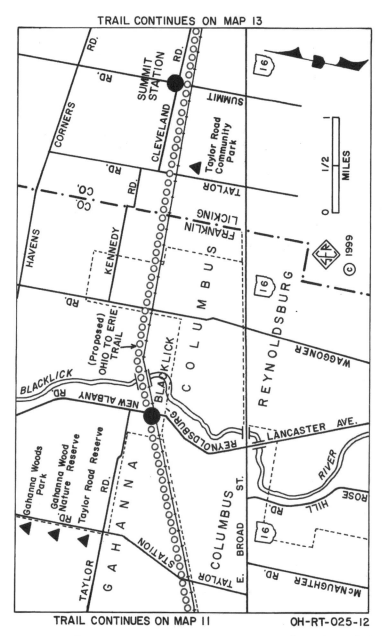

TRAIL CONTINUES ON MAP 13

TRAIL CONTINUES ON MAP 11   OH-RT-025-12

OHIO TO ERIE TRAIL (MAP 12)
FRANKLIN & LICKING COUNTIES

A RAIL-TRAIL NEARBY (MAP 13)
OHIO CANAL GREENWAY

VICINITY: *Newark*
TRAIL LENGTH: *3.0 Miles*
SURFACE: *Ballast*
TRAIL USE:

Even though this trail will not be part of the Ohio to Erie Trail, the Ohio Canal Greenway is not very far away. This trail utilizes both an old rail line and the canal towpath. The trail goes from US Route-40 in Hebron to State Route-79 near Buckeye Lake. A replica of a covered bridge crosses a small stream near Interstate-70. Future plans may include a smoother surface on the trail, as well as a possible connection to the Ohio to Erie Trail.

PARKING:
There are currently no designated parking areas for this trail.

A replica covered bridge takes Ohio Canal Greenway users across a small stream.

FOR MORE INFORMATION:
Licking County Parks
4309 Lancaster Rd., Granville, OH 43023
740-587-2535

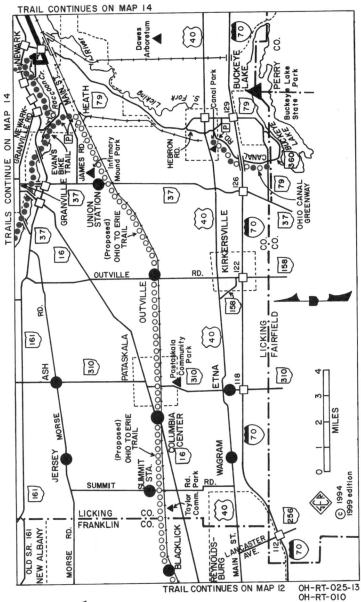

TRAIL CONTINUES ON MAP 14

TRAILS CONTINUE ON MAP 14

NEWARK

Dawes Arboretum

BUCKEYE LAKE

PERRY CO.

Buckeye Lake State Park

HEATH

Canal Park

Infirmary Mound Park

HEBRON RD.

OHIO CANAL GREENWAY

GRANVILLE

UNION STATION

(Proposed) OHIO TO ERIE TRAIL

KIRKERSVILLE

OUTVILLE

OUTVILLE RD.

PATASKALA

Pataskala Community Park

ETNA

LICKING FAIRFIELD

ASH

(Proposed) OHIO TO ERIE TRAIL

COLUMBIA CENTER

WAGRAM

JERSEY

SUMMIT

SUMMIT STA.

Taylor Rd. Comm. Park

LICKING CO.
FRANKLIN CO.

BLACKLICK

NEW ALBANY

REYNOLDS-BURG

MILES

© 1994
1999 edition

TRAIL CONTINUES ON MAP 12

OH-RT-025-13
OH-RT-010

OHIO TO ERIE TRAIL (MAP 13)
FRANKLIN & LICKING COUNTIES
335.0 MILES (TRAIL INCOMPLETE)
SURFACE: ASPHALT

OHIO CANAL GREENWAY
LICKING COUNTY
3.0 MILES; SURFACE: BALLAST

JOHNSTOWN-NEWARK-HANOVER SECTION (MAPS 14 AND 15)
EVANS (THOMAS J.) BIKE TRAIL
VICINITY: *Newark*
TRAIL LENGTH: *18.8 and 8.5 Miles*
SURFACE: *Asphalt*
TRAIL USE: 🚴 🚵 🚶 ♿ 🐎 ⛷ 🏃

The Evans Bike Trail traverses Licking County from west to east. Currently, the trail has two separate sections; Johnstown to Newark, and "The Panhandle" east of Newark. The Evans Bike Trail is also part of the Ohio to Erie Trail.

Known as the Johnstown-Newark Bike Trail to many residents of Central Ohio, the Thomas J. Evans Bike Trail provides trail users with a great escape from the fast-paced lifestyle. Most of this trail parallels Raccoon Creek through the Licking County countryside, offering users a variety of pastoral scenery, including farms, thick woods, colorful meadows and long green canopies of trees. Users enjoy flat and wooded terrain towards Johnstown, and a gradual five-mile decent provides an almost effortless ride from Johnstown to Alexandria. The trail scenery remains somewhat hilly beyond Alexandria before becoming very hilly near Newark. Historic Granville, with its beautifully restored homes, old-fashioned inns, boutiques, ice cream parlors and Denison University, is a nice place to stop. The rail-trail ends just west of Newark on Main Street and James Road. However, the Evan's trail continues east of Cherry Valley Road and follows the Raccoon River.

From the Cherry Valley Lodge, the bike path parallels State Route-16 to the YMCA on Church Street and connects to the O.S.U. Newark Campus. Streets can be easily taken east from this trail through downtown Newark to reach the Panhandle Section.

East of downtown Newark's courthouse along East Main Street, this section of the Evans Bike Trail is known as the Panhandle Trail, which parallels the Panhandle Line. The 8.5-mile trail goes from the North Licking River on East Main Street in Newark, through Hanover to Fellumlee Road, near the Muskingum-Licking County Line.

PARKING:
Parking can be found in the cities of Johnstown, Alexandria, Newark, Marne and Fellumlee Road.

FOR MORE INFORMATION:
Thomas J. Evans Foundation
P.O. Box 4217, Newark, OH 43058
740-349-8276

Licking County Parks
P.O. Box 590
Granville, OH 43023
740-587-2535

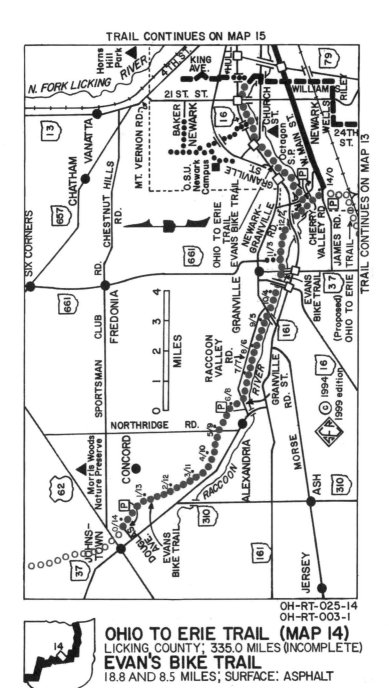

TRAIL CONTINUES ON MAP 15

N. FORK LICKING

Horns Hill Park

RIVER

4TH ST.

KING AVE.

HULL

79

21 ST. ST.

WILLIAMS

RILEY

13

VANATTA

MT. VERNON RD.

BAKER

NEWARK

16

Octagon

CHURCH ST.

S.P. R.R.

W. MAIN ST.

NEWARK

WELLS

24TH ST.

CHATHAM

CHESTNUT HILLS RD.

O.S.U. Newark Campus

GRANVILLE ST.

14/0

P

CHERRY VALLEY RD.

TRAIL CONTINUES ON MAP 13

657

NEWARK–GRANVILLE RD.

12/2

11/3

OHIO TO ERIE TRAIL EVANS BIKE TRAIL

JAMES RD.

P

SIX CORNERS

CHESTNUT HILLS RD.

661

37

EVANS BIKE TRAIL

(Proposed) OHIO TO ERIE TRAIL

661

FREDONIA

GRANVILLE RD.

SPORTSMAN CLUB

4

3

2

1

MILES

0

RACCOON VALLEY RD.

10/4

9/5

8/6

7/7

161

161

6

© 1994

1999 edition

GRANVILLE RD. ST.

NORTHRIDGE RD.

P

6/8

5/9

RIVER

MORSE

Morris Woods Nature Preserve

CONCORD

4/10

3/11

RACCOON

ALEXANDRIA

62

P

2/12

1/13

310

ASH

310

JOHNS-TOWN

0/14

P

DUGL. AVE.

EVANS BIKE TRAIL

310

161

37

JERSEY

OH-RT-025-14
OH-RT-003-1

OHIO TO ERIE TRAIL (MAP 14)
LICKING COUNTY; 335.0 MILES (INCOMPLETE)
EVAN'S BIKE TRAIL
18.8 AND 8.5 MILES; SURFACE: ASPHALT

14

A RAIL-TRAIL NEARBY (MAP 15)
BLACKHAND GORGE TRAIL
VICINITY: *Newark*
TRAIL LENGTH: *4.5 Miles*
SURFACE: *Asphalt*
TRAIL USE: 🚲 🛴 🚶 🦽 🏇 ⛷ ♿

The Ohio & Erie Canal, Central Ohio Railroad and interurban electric lines near Newark were abandoned by 1929, and only traces of them can be found today in this valley. In 1975 the Blackhand Gorge State Nature Preserve was opened. Today the preserve offers scientific, educational and recreational opportunities. The name comes from the sandstone formation in which a narrow east-west gorge was cut through by the Licking River. It also plays host to the Blackhand Gorge Trail, one of Ohio's most spectacular rail-trails.

The 4.5-mile Blackhand Gorge Trail consists of an asphalt surface and follows the old Central Ohio Railroad grade. All types of trail users can enjoy this wonderful 4.5-mile trail. Its east end clearly displays the rock exposed as workers cut a path for the old railroad. Many foot paths connect with the main Blackhand Gorge Trail, offering hikers an opportunity to further explore the scenic valley. Future plans are to connect this trail to the Ohio to Erie Trail. For more information, write to the address below.

PARKING:
Parking can be found on each end of the trail.

The Blackhand Gorge Trail cuts through the Blackhand Rock formation.

FOR MORE INFORMATION:
Ohio Dept. of Natural Resources
1889 Fountain Square, F-1,
Columbus, OH 43224
614-265-6464

Ohio Dept. of Natural Resources
5213 Rock Haven Rd., SE, Newark,
OH 43055
740-763-4411

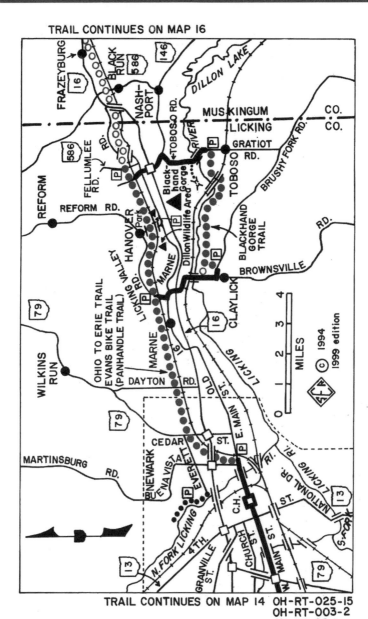

TRAIL CONTINUES ON MAP 16

TRAIL CONTINUES ON MAP 14   OH-RT-025-15
OH-RT-003-2
OH-RT-004

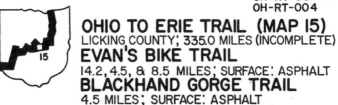

OHIO TO ERIE TRAIL (MAP 15)
LICKING COUNTY; 335.0 MILES (INCOMPLETE)
EVAN'S BIKE TRAIL
14.2, 4.5, & 8.5 MILES; SURFACE: ASPHALT
BLACKHAND GORGE TRAIL
4.5 MILES; SURFACE: ASPHALT

HANOVER-COSHOCTON SECTION (MAPS 16 AND 17)

In the future, the Evans Bike Trail in Licking County will continue northeast through Muskingum and Coshocton Counties to the City of Coshocton passing through Frazeysburg, Trinway, Dresden, Adams Mills and Conesville. In Muskingum County, attractions consist of the Dillon Wildlife Area near Nashport, and the home of the Longaberger Family basket business in Dresden. In addition to the restaurants, shops and boutiques in Dresden, the Muskingum Recreational Trail will connect to this section of the Ohio to Erie Trail. Just outside Coshocton is the famous historical Roscoe Village, where artisans demonstrate old-time crafts. Also, visitors can take a cruise on the Ohio & Erie Canal in a horse drawn canal boat.

Eastern Licking County has a "Rails with Trail" along the Ohio to Erie Trail.

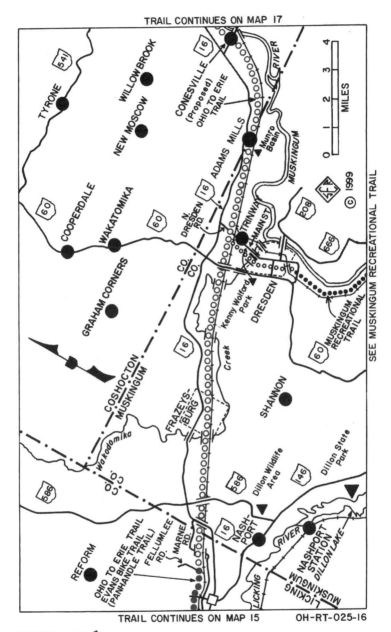

TRAIL CONTINUES ON MAP 17

TYRONE

WILLOW BROOK

NEW MOSCOW

CONESVILLE (Proposed) OHIO TO ERIE TRAIL

RIVER

ADAMS MILLS

MUSKINGUM

Munro Basin

© 1999

COOPERDALE

WAKATOMIKA

N. DRESDEN RD.

TRINWAY

MAIN ST.

SEE MUSKINGUM RECREATIONAL TRAIL

GRAHAM CORNERS

CO. CO.

Kenny Wolford Park

DRESDEN

MUSKINGUM RECREATIONAL TRAIL

COSHOCTON MUSKINGUM

Creek

SHANNON

Wakatomika

FRAZEYS- BURG

CO. CO.

Dillon State Park

Dillon Wildlife Area

REFORM

OHIO TO ERIE TRAIL EVANS BIKE TRAIL (PANHANDLE TRAIL)

FELLUMLEE RD.

MARNE RD.

NASH- PORT

LICKING RIVER

NASHPORT STATION DILLON LAKE

MUSKINGUM

LICKING

MILES

0 1 2 3 4

TRAIL CONTINUES ON MAP 15   OH-RT-025-16

OHIO TO ERIE TRAIL (MAP 16)
LICKING, MUSKINGUM, & COSHOCTON COUNTIES
335.0 MILES (TRAIL INCOMPLETE)

COSHOCTON SECTION (MAP 17)
COSHOCTON TO LAKE PARK BIKE PATH
VICINITY: *Coshocton*
TRAIL LENGTH: *3.0 Miles*
SURFACE: *Asphalt*
TRAIL USE:

The Coshocton-Lake Park Bike Path starts on Bridge Street in Coshocton and winds its way up the Walhonding River towards Lake Park. The three-mile bike path also intersects with the Ohio & Erie Canal Towpath Trail where folks can still travel the canal in a horse drawn canal boat. The Ohio & Erie Canal Towpath Trail goes south to the historical Roscoe Village. Plans are for the Coshocton-Lake Park Bike Path to be extended an additional 20 miles to complete Coshocton County's section of the Ohio to Erie Trail.

PARKING:
Parking can be found in Lake Park and Roscoe Village.

COSHOCTON-ZOARVILLE (MAPS 17, 18 AND 19)
From Coshocton to Zoarville, plans are in the works to follow the abandoned railroad from Coshocton to Newcomerstown passing through West Lafayette. Another abandoned rail corridor will be used to take trail users from Newcomerstown to New Philadelphia passing through Stone Creek and Joyce. A highlight to this trail will be a refurbished railroad tunnel seven miles north of Newcomerstown. Since Interstate-77 severs the old railroad grade near New Philadelphia, back streets will be used through the city of Dover. A third railroad corridor following the Tuscarawas River will take trail users between Dover and Zoarville before reaching the historical Towpath Trail along the Ohio & Erie Canal.

FOR MORE INFORMATION:
Coshocton City and Co. Rec. Team
45618 County Rd. 58,
Coshocton, OH 43812
740-622-3791

Friends of the Parks
23253 State Route 83,
Coshocton, OH 43812
No Phone #

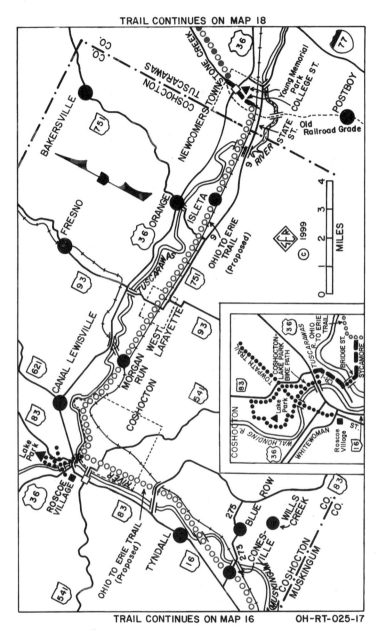

TRAIL CONTINUES ON MAP 18

TRAIL CONTINUES ON MAP 16   OH-RT-025-17

OHIO TO ERIE TRAIL (MAP 17)
COSHOCTON & TUSCARAWAS COUNTIES
COSHOCTON-LAKE PARK
BIKE PATH

The Evan's Bike Trail.

The Evan's Bike Trail is a section of the Ohio to Erie Trail.

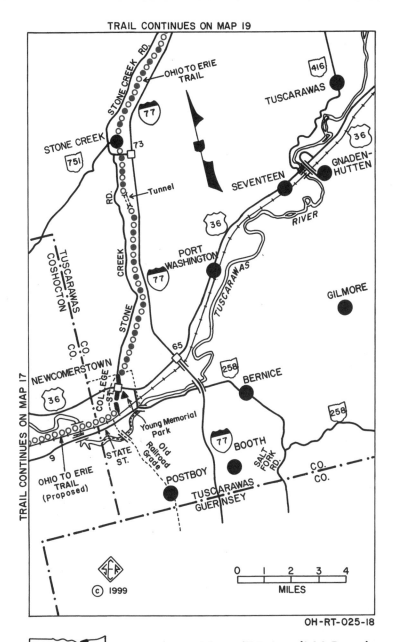

TRAIL CONTINUES ON MAP 19

OHIO TO ERIE TRAIL

STONE CREEK RD.

77

TUSCARAWAS

416

36

STONE CREEK

751

73

GNADEN-HUTTEN

Tunnel

SEVENTEEN

RD.

36

RIVER

GILMORE

TUSCARAWAS COSHOCTON CO.

PORT WASHINGTON

77

TUSCARAWAS

STONE CREEK

65

NEWCOMERSTOWN

258

BERNICE

258

36

COLLEGE ST.

Young Memorial Park

77

BOOTH

SALT FORK RD.

CO. CO.

9

STATE ST.

Old Railroad Grade

OHIO TO ERIE TRAIL (Proposed)

POSTBOY

TUSCARAWAS GUERNSEY

TRAIL CONTINUES ON MAP 17

© 1999

0 1 2 3 4
MILES

OH-RT-025-18

OHIO TO ERIE TRAIL (MAP 18)
COSHOCTON & TUSCARAWAS COUNTIES

18

ZOARVILLE-CLEVELAND SECTION (MAPS 19, 20, 21, 22, 23 AND 24)
TOWPATH TRAIL (Ohio-Erie)

VICINITY: *Zoarville/Massillon/Akron/Cleveland*
TRAIL LENGTH: *87.0 Miles (Trail Incomplete)*
SURFACE: *Asphalt and Smooth Crushed Gravel*
TRAIL USE: 🚲 🏇 🚶 ⛺ 🐎 ⛷ 🚶 *(Bridal Path in Stark County)*

The 87-mile Towpath Trail is part of the Ohio to Erie Trail. Currently, sections are open for trail use including bicycles through Stark, Summit and Cuyahoga Counties. From Zoarville to Akron, the Towpath Trail follows the Tuscarawas River; from Akron to Cleveland, the Towpath Trail follows the Cuyahoga River. Akron is on the Towpath's drainage divide, giving Summit County its name. At one time the canal ran 309 miles from the Ohio River in Portsmouth to Lake Erie in Cleveland. Mule-pulled boats traveled it for almost ninety years between 1825 and 1913. Presently, the northern 87 miles are being reopened to a new form of transportation. When complete, trail users will be able to travel from Zoarville to Cleveland's Lake Erie shore.

The "Looking Back" painting on a building in downtown Massillon by artist Eric Alan Grohe reflects on Massillon's canal history.

FOR MORE INFORMATION:
Cleveland to Zoarville:
Ohio & Erie Canal Corridor Coalition
520 S. Main St., Suite 2541-F
Akron, OH 44311
330-434-5657

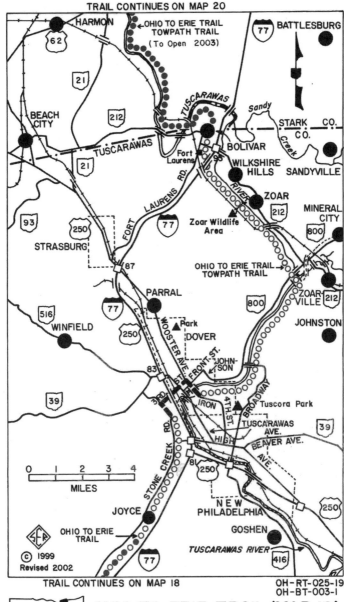

TRAIL CONTINUES ON MAP 20

OHIO TO ERIE TRAIL
TOWPATH TRAIL
(To Open 2003)

HARMON

BATTLESBURG

BEACH CITY

STARK CO.

STARK CO.

TUSCARAWAS

Fort Laurens

BOLIVAR

WILKSHIRE HILLS

SANDYVILLE

ZOAR

Sandy Creek

Zoar Wildlife Area

MINERAL CITY

STRASBURG

OHIO TO ERIE TRAIL TOWPATH TRAIL

ZOAR-VILLE

PARRAL

JOHNSTON

WINFIELD

DOVER

Park

JOHN-SON

Tuscora Park

TUSCARAWAS AVE.

BEAVER AVE.

MILES

0 1 2 3 4

JOYCE

OHIO TO ERIE TRAIL

NEW PHILADELPHIA

GOSHEN

© 1999
Revised 2002

TUSCARAWAS RIVER

TRAIL CONTINUES ON MAP 18

OH-RT-025-19
OH-BT-003-1

OHIO TO ERIE TRAIL (MAP 19)
TUSCARAWAS & STARK COUNTIES
TOWPATH TRAIL (OHIO & ERIE)
86.0 MILES (TRAIL INCOMPLETE)
SURFACE: CONCRETE, ASPHALT, & SMOOTH CRUSHED GRAVEL

TUSCARAWAS COUNTY

The Towpath Trail starts in Zoarville northeast of New Philadelphia, and goes north through Tuscarawas County passing through Zoar, Wilkshire Hills and Bolivar; Zoar's Wildlife Area and Fort Laurens are two highlights along this part of the trail. Unfortunately, no trail improvements have been made in Trumbull County during this time.

PARKING:

No parking places have been established.

STARK COUNTY

Two sections of the Towpath Trail are open in Stark County. The first section goes from Bolivar on State Route-212 to the River Levee in Massillon. Through Navarre, Canal Street must be followed. The second section of trail starts on Towpath Court off Erie Avenue in the north end of Massillon and goes 15 miles north to Clinton passing through Canal Fulton and Crystal Springs. Canal Fulton's section of the Towpath Trail offers mule-driven canal boat tours along the Ohio & Erie Canal. The trail surface for all of Stark County's Towpath Trail consists of smooth crushed gravel; Massillon's section will consist of an asphalt surface when complete.

PARKING:

Parking can be found in Navarre, Massillon, Crystal Spring and Canal Fulton.

Mule powered tow boats still operate in Canal-Fulton along the Towpath Trail.

FOR MORE INFORMATION:
Stark County:
Stark County Park District
5300 Tyner Avenue NW, Canton, OH 44708
330-477-3552

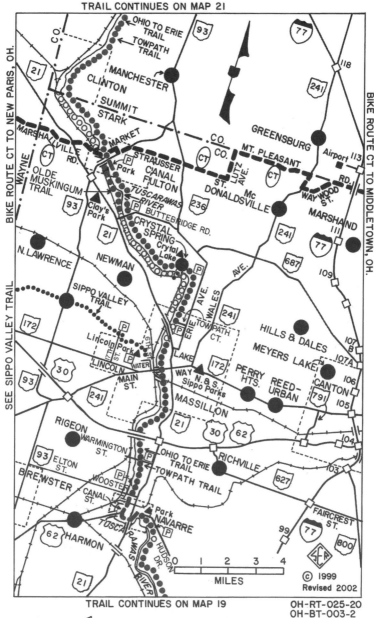

TRAIL CONTINUES ON MAP 21

OHIO TO ERIE TRAIL

TOWPATH TRAIL

BIKE ROUTE CT TO NEW PARIS, OH.

BIKE ROUTE CT TO MIDDLETOWN, OH.

MANCHESTER

CLINTON

SUMMIT
STARK

MARKET

MARSHALLVILLE RD.

STRAUSSER

P Park

CANAL FULTON

OLDE MUSKINGUM TRAIL

Clay's Park

TUSCARAWAS RIVER

BUTTERBRIDGE RD.

CRYSTAL SPRING

Crystal Lake

GREENSBURG

MT. PLEASANT

Airport 113

DONALDSVILLE

Mc

LUTZ AVE.

WAYWOOD ST.

MARSHAND 111

N. LAWRENCE

NEWMAN

SIPPO VALLEY TRAIL

SEE SIPPO VALLEY TRAIL

Lincoln Park

LINCOLN

MAIN ST.

WATER

LAKE

ERIE AVE.

WALES AVE.

Towpath CT.

WAY N. & S. Sippo Parks

MASSILLON

HILLS & DALES

MEYERS LAKE

PERRY HTS.

REED-URBAN

CANTON

RIGEON

WARMINGTON ST.

ELTON ST.

BREWSTER

WOOSTER

CANAL ST.

NAVARRE

Park

TUSCARAWAS RIVER

HUDSON DR.

HARMON

OHIO TO ERIE TRAIL

TOWPATH TRAIL

RICHVILLE

FAIRCREST ST.

© 1999
Revised 2002

MILES

0 1 2 3 4

TRAIL CONTINUES ON MAP 19

OH-RT-025-20
OH-BT-003-2

20

OHIO TO ERIE TRAIL (MAP 20)
STARK & SUMMIT COUNTIES

TOWPATH TRAIL (OHIO & ERIE)
OLDE MUSKINGUM TRAIL
2.0 MILES; SMOOTH CRUSHED GRAVEL

SUMMIT COUNTY

The Towpath Trail follows the Ohio & Erie Canal through Summit County from south to north passing through Franklin-Clinton, Barberton, Akron and the Cuyahoga Valley National Recreation Area (C.V.N.R.A.). Even though the Towpath Trail has yet to be developed through the southern part of Summit County, the Towpath Trail can be enjoyed from Akron to the Cuyahoga Valley National Recreation Area. Two sections of the Towpath Trail have been developed through Clinton and Barberton.

Several very short sections of the Towpath Trail have been developed through downtown Akron, bringing the canal heritage back to the business districts of Akron. The trail surface varies from asphalt to concrete, brick and stone. Cyclists can enjoy a section in the south end of Akron from Summit Lake Park to Bartges Street; several city parks align this section. Other very short segments are being developed through the downtown area. Just north of Exchange Street is a monument with facts about the canal boats. Just north of downtown Akron on North Street, a much longer section of the Towpath Trail goes through northern Akron and connects directly with both the C.V.N.R.A. and Cleveland's sections of the Towpath Trail; this entire section is 32 miles.

PARKING:

Parking is available south of downtown Akron in Summit Lake Park. In the northern part of Akron parking is found on Memorial Parkway, Merriman Road and the C.V.N.R.A. parking lot on Riverview Road.

Gardens and parks align the Towpath Trail through Akron.

FOR MORE INFORMATION:
Summit County:
Summit County Metroparks
975 Treaty Line Rd., Akron, OH 44313
330-867-5511

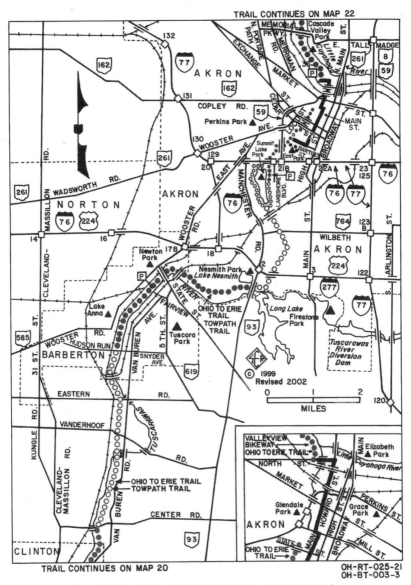

TRAIL CONTINUES ON MAP 22

TRAIL CONTINUES ON MAP 20

OH-RT-025-21
OH-BT-003-3

OHIO TO ERIE TRAIL (MAP 21)
SUMMIT COUNTY
TOWPATH TRAIL (OHIO & ERIE)

CUYAHOGA VALLEY NATIONAL RECREATION AREA

The Towpath Trail follows the Ohio & Erie Canal through the Cuyahoga Valley National Recreation Area (C.V.N.R.A.). The mile markers are based on those once used by canal travelers. These markers, including mile marker 0 at Lake Erie in downtown Cleveland, serve as a reminder of the canal and provide Towpath Trail users with a unique way to gauge the distance they've traveled. Going from south to north, the mile markers decrease while trail users get closer to Lake Erie.

This smooth crushed gravel trail starts in Summit County just south of Bath Road at mile post 30 and runs all the way into Cuyahoga County on Rockside Road at mile post 11, taking users from Akron to Cleveland and passing through the center of the Cuyahoga Valley National Recreation Area as it parallels the Cuyahoga River.

From Bath Road (mile post 30) to Ira Road (mile post 28), the old canal was destroyed while constructing Riverview Road, and only remnants of a few locks remain along this stretch of the Towpath Trail. From Ira Road, the trail passes the Hale Farm and Village (mile post 28) and goes over an expanse of wetland on a wooden-decked bridge to Peninsula where antique shops, stores and restaurants can be enjoyed (mile post 24). Active passenger excursion trains pass through Peninsula from Akron to Cleveland (for more information on the train excursions, write to the address on page 98).

The Towpath Trail traverses wetlands as a boardwalk (near mile posts 27 and 28).

Continuing north, the Towpath Trail takes users from Peninsula to Boston Mills Road near mile post 21, where there is a youth hostel (See addresses for hostels on page 175). Between Peninsula and Boston, the trail becomes a long wood-decked "bridge" to traverse a large forested wetland. The trail also passes under the Ohio Turnpike (Interstate-80) and under the Interstate-271 bridges on its way to Boston, where a canal museum is located.

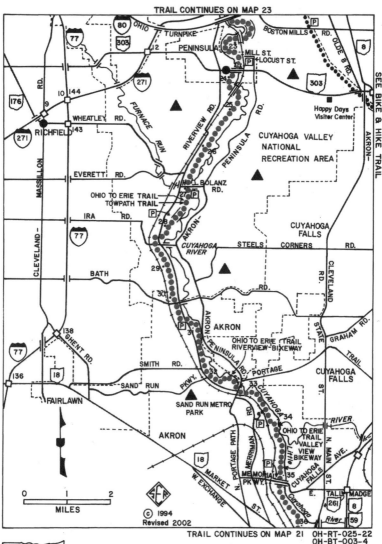

TRAIL CONTINUES ON MAP 23

PENINSULA

CUYAHOGA VALLEY
NATIONAL
RECREATION AREA

Happy Days
Visiter Center

OHIO TO ERIE TRAIL
TOWPATH TRAIL

CUYAHOGA
FALLS

CUYAHOGA
RIVER

AKRON

OHIO TO ERIE TRAIL
RIVERVIEW-BIKEWAY

CUYAHOGA
FALLS

SAND RUN METRO
PARK

OHIO TO ERIE
TRAIL
VALLEY
VIEW
BIKEWAY

AKRON

FAIRLAWN

RICHFIELD

WHEATLEY RD.

FURNACE RUN

EVERETT RD.

IRA RD.

BATH

GHENT RD.

SMITH RD.

SAND RUN

MASSILLON

CLEVELAND —

RIVERVIEW RD.

PENINSULA RD.

MILL ST.
LOCUST ST.

BOSTON MILLS RD.

OLDE 8 RD.

AKRON-

SEE BIKE & HIKE TRAIL

STEELS CORNERS RD.

CLEVELAND RD.

STATE RD.

GRAHAM RD.

N. MAIN AVE.

CUYAHOGA FALLS ST.

RIVER

TALLMADGE

E. Cuyahoga River

PORTAGE PATH

N. PORTAGE PATH

MERRIMAN RD.

MEMORIAL PKWY.

W. EXCHANGE ST.

MARKET

Little Cuyahoga

0   1   2
MILES

© 1994
Revised 2002

TRAIL CONTINUES ON MAP 2I   OH-RT-025-22
                              OH-BT-003-4

OHIO TO ERIE TRAIL (MAP 22)
SUMMIT COUNTY

TOWPATH TRAIL (OHIO & ERIE)

Another two miles north, near mile post 19, the Towpath Trail intersects with the Old Carriage Trail, which leads up a long hill to connect with the 29- mile Bike & Hike Trail to either Bedford or Kent. Most of the canal beds lie empty or have become wetlands and home to an abundance of wildlife throughout this area. Near mile post 17, the Towpath Trail intersects with the Emerald Necklace Trail which goes west to Brecksville through the Brecksville Reservation. From State Route-82 to Rockside Road, water still runs through the canal, and trail users can see old locks and aqueducts operate. At mile post 12, the Canal Visitor Center offers visitors historic information, locks demonstration and a museum, making it a great place to stop and visit along the trail. From Rockside Road (mile post 11), the Towpath Trail continues north into Cleveland.

PARKING:
Parking is available in Akron near Bath Road, places along Riverview Road, Peninsula, Boston, Highland Road, Chippewa Creek Drive, the Canal Visitor Center (mile post 12), and Rockside Road.

The Towpath Trail follows the old Ohio & Erie Canal (mile post 12).

FOR MORE INFORMATION:
Cuyahoga Valley N.R.A.:
Cuyahoga Valley National Rec. Area
15610 Vaughn Rd., Brecksville, OH 44141
216-526-5256

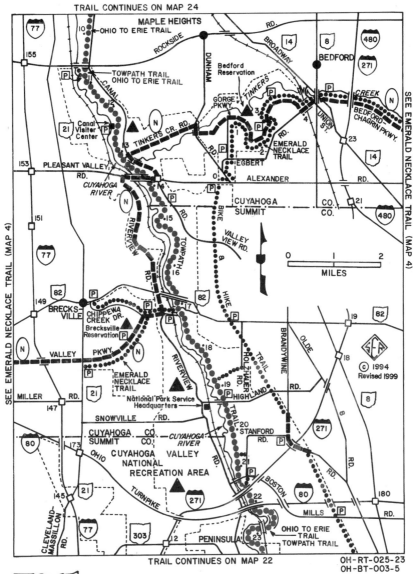

TRAIL CONTINUES ON MAP 24

MAPLE HEIGHTS

OHIO TO ERIE TRAIL

77

155

ROCKSIDE RD.

BROADWAY

14

8

480

BEDFORD

271

TOWPATH TRAIL
OHIO TO ERIE TRAIL

DUNHAM

Bedford
Reservation

GORGE PKWY.

TINKERS

CREEK

BEDFORD
CHAGRIN PKWY.

N

Canal
Visiter
Center

21

TINKERS CR. RD.

EMERALD
NECKLACE
TRAIL

UNION ST.

23

14

153

PLEASANT VALLEY RD.

EGBERT

ALEXANDER RD.

CO.
CO.

21

CUYAHOGA RIVER

CUYAHOGA
SUMMIT

480

151

BIKE

VALLEY
VIEW RD.

0   1   2
MILES

77

RIVERVIEW RD.

TOWPATH TRAIL

HIKE

82

82

BRECKS-VILLE

CHIPPEWA CREEK DR.

Brecksville
Reservation

82

19

SCA
© 1994
Revised 1999

VALLEY PKWY.

N

EMERALD
NECKLACE
TRAIL

RIVERVIEW

HOLZHAUER TRAIL

BRANDYWINE

OLDE RD.

18

8

MILLER RD.

21

National Park Service
Headquarters

HIGHLAND TRAIL

271

8

147

SNOWVILLE RD.

CUYAHOGA CO.
SUMMIT CO.

CUYAHOGA
RIVER

STANFORD RD.

80

173

OHIO

CUYAHOGA
NATIONAL
RECREATION AREA

271

BOSTON

80

180

145

21

TURNPIKE

77

303

PENINSULA

MILLS RD.

OHIO TO ERIE
TRAIL
TOWPATH TRAIL

CLEVELAND-MASSILLON RD.

TRAIL CONTINUES ON MAP 22

OH-RT-025-23
OH-BT-003-5

23

OHIO TO ERIE TRAIL (MAP 23)
SUMMIT & CUYAHOGA COUNTIES

TOWPATH TRAIL (OHIO & ERIE)

CUYAHOGA COUNTY

This section of the Towpath Trail is a unique blend of both nature and man-made structures from the industrial age, and is maintained by the Cleveland Metroparks. The mile markers are also based on those once used by canal travelers. These markers, including marker 0 at Lake Erie in downtown Cleveland, serve as a reminder of the canal and provide Towpath Trail users with a unique way to gauge the distance they've traveled.

From Rockside Road near mile post 11, this trail connects to the Cuyahoga Valley National Recreation Area. Between Rockside Road and Interstate-480, recreational facilities, restaurants and market places can be visited. The Towpath Trail goes under many high bridges including Interstate-480 (mile post 10), Interstate-77 (mile post 8) and the CSX Railroad Bridge (mile post 7). Many overlooks can be taken advantage of; each one has a different theme, such as the Family Farming Overlook, the Migration Overlook and the Petroleum Storage Overlook. Near mile post 7, a trail spur goes up a big hill to the Canal Way Center building, which serves as the northern terminus of the 87-mile Ohio & Erie Canal National Heritage Corridor. From mile post 7, the trail continues north to Harvard Avenue.

PARKING:

Parking is found on Rockside Road in Valley View and East 49th Street in Cleveland Heights.

The Towpath Trail blends both the natural and industrial flavors in Cleveland.

FOR MORE INFORMATION:

Cuyahoga County:
Cleveland Metroparks
4101 Fulton Parkway, Cleveland, OH 44144
216-351-6300

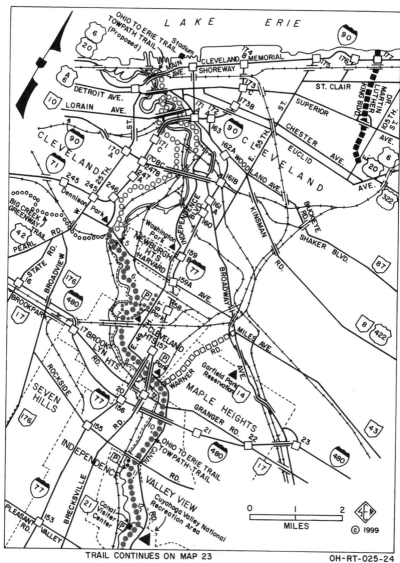

TRAIL CONTINUES ON MAP 23

OH-RT-025-24
OH-BT-003-6

OHIO TO ERIE TRAIL (MAP 24)
CUYAHOGA COUNTY

TOWPATH TRAIL (OHIO & ERIE)

HEADWATERS TRAIL

VICINITY: *Garrettsville*
TRAIL LENGTH: *7.0 Miles*
SURFACE: *Smooth Crushed Gravel and Back Roads*
TRAIL USE:

The Headwater's Trail is a 7 mile rail-trail traversing the scenic fields and forests of northern Portage County and connecting the historic villages of Mantua and Garrettsville. The rail-trail gets its name from a geological formation. Even though the rail-trail appears level, it crosses a continental drainage divide; water flowing to the north goes into the Great Lakes, and water flowing to the south goes into the Gulf of Mexico.

The trail starts in Village Park on High Street in Mantua and goes three miles east to Asbury Road. From there, a break in the railroad corridor causes trail users to follow bike route signs along 1.5 miles of back roads to Hiram Station, located on State Route-700. From the Hiram Station Parking Lot, the rail-trail goes another three miles east to the Village Park Library in Garrettsville.

PARKING:
Parking is Available in Mantua, Hiram Station and Garrettsville.

A trail head sign for the Headwaters Trail.

FOR MORE INFORMATION:

Portage County Park District
449 Meridian St., Ravenna, OH 44266
330-673-9404

Headwaters Land Trust
P.O. Box 171
Hiram, OH 44234

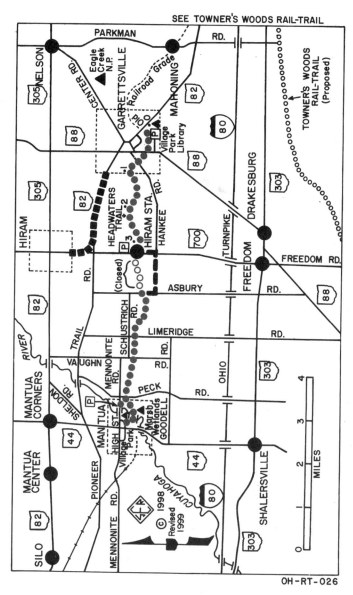

SEE TOWNER'S WOODS RAIL-TRAIL

OH-RT-026

HEADWATERS TRAIL
PORTAGE COUNTY
7.0 MILES
SURFACE: SMOOTH CRUSHED GRAVEL

LESTER RAIL-TRAIL

VICINITY: *Medina*
TRAIL LENGTH: *3.2 Miles*
SURFACE: *Smooth Crushed Gravel*
TRAIL USE:

CHIPPEWA RAIL-TRAIL

VICINITY: *Medina*
TRAIL LENGTH: *5.0 Miles*
SURFACE: *Ballast*
TRAIL USE:

LESTER RAIL-TRAIL

The Lester Rail-Trail begins in Lester and goes 3.2 miles southeast to Abbeyville Road. Nature can be readily enjoyed along this trail, and most of the scenery is wooded. Between Fenn Road and Abbeyville Road, a trail spur goes south to the Media County Career Center.

PARKING:

Parking is found in Lester and the Medina County Career Center Parking Lot.

CHIPPEWA RAIL-TRAIL

The Chippewa Rail-Trail goes from Ryan Road in Medina, to Chippewa Road. The wooded areas and ravines along this trail add beauty. At this time, the surface is not suitable for touring bicycles. Future plans are to improve this trail surface with smooth crushed gravel and to connect the Chippewa Rail-Trail with the Lester Rail-Rail through the City of Medina.

PARKING:

Currently no parking places have been established.

Walkers enjoy a stroll down by the Lester Rail-Trail.

FOR MORE INFORMATION:
Medina County Park District
6364 Deerview Lane, Medina, OH 44256
330-722-9364

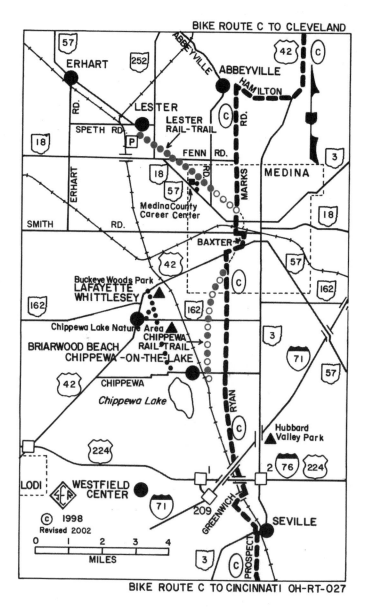

BIKE ROUTE C TO CLEVELAND

57
ERHART
252
ABBEYVILLE
42
C
LESTER
LESTER
RAIL-TRAIL
C
ABBEYVILLE
HAMILTON
RD.
SPETH RD.
P
18
FENN RD.
RD.
3
18
MARKS
57
MEDINA
Medina County
Career Center
18
SMITH   RD.
BAXTER
42
57
Buckeye Woods Park
LAFAYETTE
WHITTLESEY
C
162
162
Chippewa Lake Nature Area
CHIPPEWA
RAIL-TRAIL
3
71
BRIARWOOD BEACH
CHIPPEWA-ON-THE-LAKE
57
42
CHIPPEWA
Chippewa Lake
RYAN
C
Hubbard
Valley Park
224
2 76 224
LODI
WESTFIELD
CENTER
71
209
GREENWICH
SEVILLE
© 1998
Revised 2002
0   1   2   3   4
MILES
PROSPECT
3
C

BIKE ROUTE C TO CINCINNATI OH-RT-027

LESTER/CHIPPEWA RAIL-TRAILS
MEDINA COUNTY
3.2 & 5.0 MILES
SURFACE: SMOOTH CRUSHED
GRAVEL

NATIONAL ROAD BIKEWAY

VICINITY: *St. Clairsville*
TRAIL LENGTH: *2.5 Miles*
SURFACE: *Asphalt*
TRAIL USE: 🚲 🛴 🚶 🏕️ 🐎 ⛷️ ♿

The National Road Bikeway is more than just a short rail-trail through St. Clairsville. Even though it is only 2.5 miles long, this trail connects neighborhoods, schools, historic and commercial districts and parks. The main attraction along this trail is the 532-foot long and 40-foot high tunnel under US Route-40, giving the trail its name. This is also Ohio's first rail-trail to have a tunnel. Other highlights include a 60-foot high and 340-foot long curved trestle, a Hub Park with a gazebo in the center of the trail, a connection to many of St. Clairsville's destinations and the scenic natural setting of the Appalachian Mountains.

From the north end of the trail tunnel, many steps can be taken uphill to US Route-40 for refreshments. Future plans may be to extend this trail to the Ohio River and connect with Wheeling, West Virginia's Greater Wheeling Trails.

PARKING:
Parking can be found on each end of the trail.

The 532-foot tunnel along the National Road Bikeway.

FOR MORE INFORMATION:
City Recreation Dept.
100 Fair St., St. Clairsville, OH 43950
740-695-2037

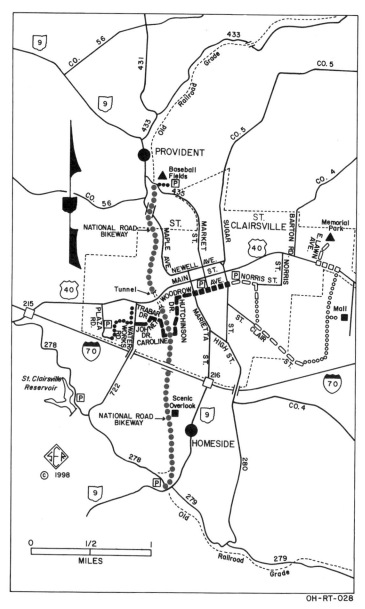

OH-RT-028

NATIONAL ROAD BIKEWAY
BELMONT COUNTY
2.5 MILES
SURFACE: ASPHALT

TRI-COUNTY TRIANGLE TRAIL

VICINITY: *Chillicothe/Washington C.H.*
TRAIL LENGTH: *52.0 Miles (Trail Incomplete)*
SURFACE: *Asphalt*
TRAIL USE: 🚲 🚵 🚶 ⛏ 🐴 ⛷ 🏃

The Tri-County Triangle Trail, also known as the "TTT" will connect three cities and three counties; Chillicothe in Ross County, Washington Court House in Fayette County, and Greenfield in Highland County. This trail will be a part of the American Discovery Trail across the United States. This trail could also connect to the Clinton Rail-Trail in Clinton County and Bike Route-3 in Greene County. Currently, three sections of the Tri-County Triangle Trail are open.

WASHINGTON C.H.

In Washington C.H., about one mile of trail has been built. The asphalt trail starts on Court Street and follows a creek along both sides to Fayette Street; the trail then goes from North Street to Elm Street where Christman Park is located. The terrain is relatively flat.

PARKING:

Parking can be found near the corner of Elm and Highland in the baseball park. It can also be found in Christman Park on Elm Street.

FRANKFORT

In Frankfort, about nine miles of trail are open. This asphalt section starts on County Road 550 and goes east along the North Fork Paint Creek. Towards Anderson the terrain is relatively hilly, scenic and most of the trail goes through wooded areas.

PARKING:

Parking can be found in Frankfort on Frankfort-Clarksburg Road and N. Mussellman Station Road.

The Tri-County Triangle Trail in Washington, C.H.

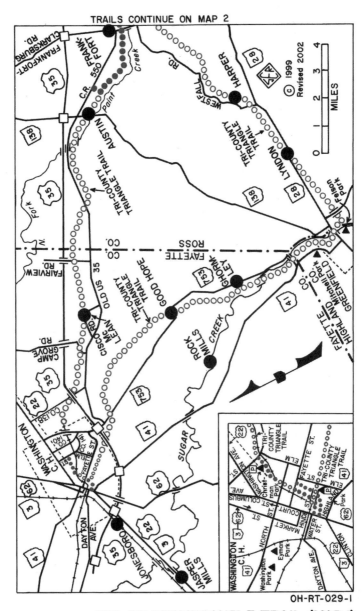

OH-RT-029-I

TRI-COUNTY TRIANGLE TRAIL (MAP I)
FAYETTE, ROSS, & HIGHLAND COUNTIES
52.0 MILES (TRAIL INCOMPLETE)
SURFACE: ASPHALT

CHILLICOTHE

In Chillicothe, 2.3 miles of the trail are open. From High Street (State Route-104) the trail goes southeast through the Park Annex of Yoctangee Park to Riverside Street. From there, the rail-trail becomes a river levee trail and follows the Scioto River from Yoctangee Park to US Route-23 and 35. The bike path dead-ends and does not connect to US Route-23 and 35.

PARKING:

Parking can be found in Chillicothe on North High Street (State Route-104), the Park Annex, Riverside Street and Poplar Street.

Future plans are to connect these three segments of the Tri-County Triangle Trail in the next three to five years between Washington C.H. and Chillicothe, and to complete the entire "Triangle" to Greenfield in the next five to ten years.

The Tri-County Triangle Trail in Chillicothe.

FOR MORE INFORMATION:

Tri-County Triangle Trail
428 Jefferson St., Greenfield, OH
45123
No Phone #

Ross County Park District
16 N. Paint St.,
Chillicothe, OH 45601
740-773-8794

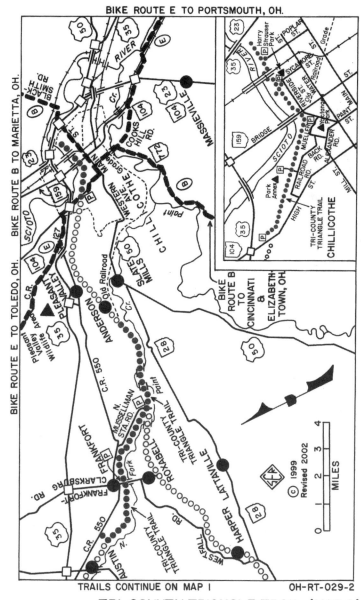

BIKE ROUTE E TO PORTSMOUTH, OH.

TRI-COUNTY TRIANGLE TRAIL (MAP 2)

TRAILS CONTINUE ON MAP 1

OH-RT-029-2

WESTERVILLE BIKEWAY

VICINITY: *Columbus*
TRAIL LENGTH: *2.3 Miles*
SURFACE: *Asphalt*
TRAIL USE:

3-C RAIL-TRAIL

VICINITY: *Columbus*
TRAIL LENGTH: *2.0 Miles*
SURFACE: *Asphalt*
TRAIL USE:

The Westerville Bikeway provides users in the northeast area of Columbus and Franklin County with a great recreational opportunity. The trail goes from south to north through the oldest sections of Westerville and passes through both Franklin and Delaware Counties. Westerville is home to Otterbein College, as well as the historical songwriter, Benjamin Russell Hanby, who wrote "Up On The House Top." Antique shops, boutiques, coffee houses, ice cream parlors and restaurants can be enjoyed along State Street (State Route-3). The 3-C Rail-Trail directly follows State Route-3 north of Westerville.

The Westerville Bikeway is part of a network of bike paths throughout Westerville and its outlying areas. Another popular bike path which has been around since the 1980s is the four-mile Sharon Woods Bike Path (Bike Route-56) which goes through the far corners of the Sharon Woods Metropark with plenty of nature and wildlife to enjoy. Future plans are to connect the Westerville Bikeway to the 3-C Rail-Trail.

PARKING:
Parking can be found on most of the back streets in Westerville along the Westerville Bikeway.

A greenway goes through Westerville.

FOR MORE INFORMATION:
City of Westerville, Dept. of Planning and Development
64 E. Walnut St., Westerville, OH 43081
614-890-8529

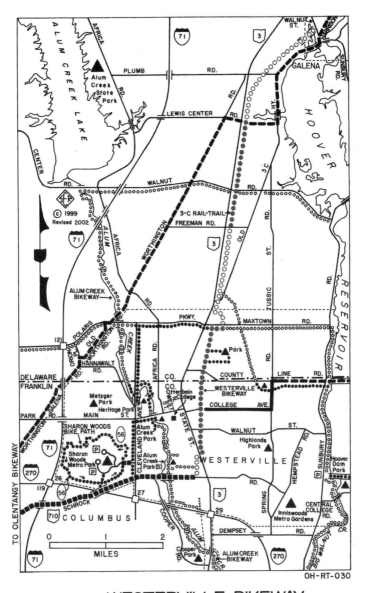

OH-RT-030

WESTERVILLE BIKEWAY
FRANKLIN & DELAWARE COUNTIES
2.3 MILES; SURFACE: ASPHALT
3-C RAIL-TRAIL
2.0 MILES; SURFACE: ASPHALT

HOLMES COUNTY RAIL-TRAIL

VICINITY: *Millersburg*
TRAIL LENGTH: *29.0 Miles (Trail Incomplete)*
SURFACE: *Gravel (Will be Asphalt with Smooth Crushed Gravel)*
TRAIL USE: 🚲 🚵 🚶 🏕 🏇 ⛷ ♿

The Holmes County Rail-Trail runs diagonally from the southwest corner to the northern edge of Holmes County. The trail roughly parallels US Route-62 from Knox County to Millersburg, and State Route-83 from Millersburg to Holmesville. From the southwest end, the Holmes County Rail-Trail starts on the northeast end of the Mohican Valley Trail near Brinkhaven and passes through Glenmont, Killbuck, Millersburg, Holmesville and the Holmes-Wayne County Line near Fredericksburg.

When complete, this trail will include a nine-foot wide asphalt bike path with a smooth crushed gravel surface for a horse and buggy path. This corridor will be the first of its kind in the United States to accommodate all trail users, including the horse and buggy. Holmes County has the largest Amish population in the United States; the Amish believe that the usage of electricity, electrical appliances and automobiles are too worldly. Therefore, the horse and buggy is their means of travel. With all of the horses, buggies and wagons using the roads and highways throughout Holmes County, the Holmes County Rail-Trail provides a unique travel option.

An Amish Buggy in Holmes County.

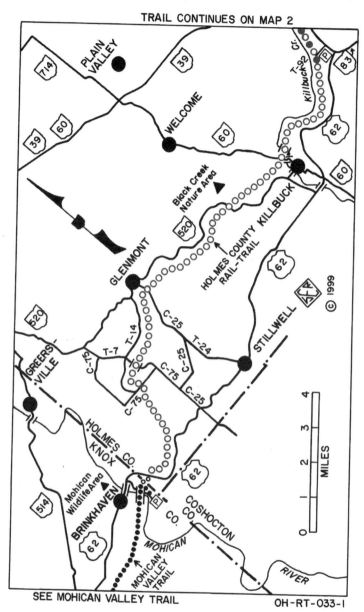

TRAIL CONTINUES ON MAP 2

PLAIN VALLEY

714

39

WELCOME

39 60

60

Black Creek Nature Area

520

GLENMONT

HOLMES COUNTY KILLBUCK RAIL-TRAIL

Killbuck Cr.

T-92

P

83

62

60

62

© 1999

520

GREERS-VILLE

T-7

T-14

C-25

C-25

C-75

C-25

T-24

STILLWELL

C-75

HOLMES CO.

KNOX

Mohican Wildlife Area

514

BRINKHAVEN

62

62

P

MOHICAN

COSHOCTON CO.

MOHICAN VALLEY TRAIL

RIVER

MILES

0 1 2 3 4

SEE MOHICAN VALLEY TRAIL

OH-RT-033-1

HOLMES COUNTY RAIL-TRAIL (MAP I)
HOLMES COUNTY
29.0 MILES; SURFACE: GRAVEL
(will be ASPHALT with GRAVEL)

Because Holmes County is one of the most desirable places to visit in Ohio, Amish communities such as Millersburg, Berlin, Charm, Walnut Creek, Winesburg, Mount Hope, Benton and Holmesville have become popular places to visit as well. Each local community's attractions vary from local bed and breakfasts, to fine Amish restaurants, traditional furniture stores, craft and quilt shops, and old-fashioned country and hardware stores. In addition to the numerous miles of scenic back roads that one can bicycle, the Holmes County Rail-Trail is handy for visitors, as well as residents for getting across Holmes County.

When complete, this 29-mile trail will continue another 18 miles southwest into Knox County on the Mohican Valley Trail and the Kokosing Gap Trail to Mount Vernon, making this rail-trail a continuous 47-miles. The Holmes County Rail-Trail may possibly be extended northeast to connect with the Sippo Valley Trail in Massillon.

PARKING:
Parking can be found in Millersburg on T-92 and just south of State-Route-39. Parking can also be found on State Route-83 just south of Holmesville.

The Holmes County Rail-Trail.

FOR MORE INFORMATION:
Holmes County Rails-to-Trails Coalition
P.O. Box 95, Millersburg, OH 44654
330-674-1643

Chamber of Commerce and Tourist Bureau
35 N. Monroe St.,
Millersburg, OH 44654
330-674-3975

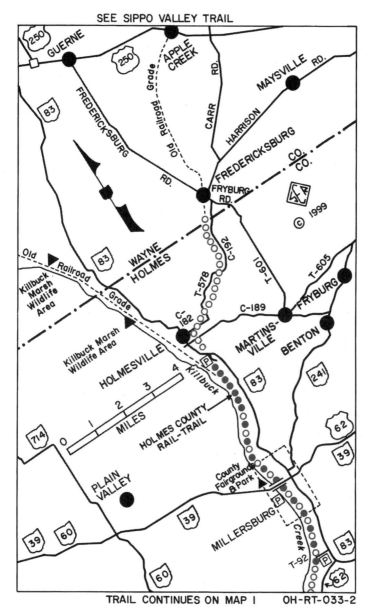

SEE SIPPO VALLEY TRAIL

TRAIL CONTINUES ON MAP I   OH-RT-033-2

HOLMES COUNTY RAIL-TRAIL
(MAP 2)

SIPPO VALLEY TRAIL

VICINITY: *Massillon*
TRAIL LENGTH: *9.0 Miles*
SURFACE: *Asphalt and Smooth Crushed Gravel*
TRAIL USE: 🚲 🛼 🚶 🪑 🐎 ⛷ 🚶

The Sippo Valley Trail goes west to east, from Dalton to Massillon. The trail gets its name from Sippo Creek, which the trail follows through Stark County. This trail roughly parallels US Route-30 on the north side.

The trail starts in Dalton near Village Green Park and North Freet Street. The trail goes east through fields and forests and over several streams towards Sippo.

In Sippo, refreshments can be found; from here, the trail goes to Belmont Avenue in Massillon. The Sippo Valley Trail then curves around and passes through Lincoln Park. The trail ends at the Lincoln playground on Water Street. Just one block away is the Tuscarawas River, and on the other side is the Ohio to Erie Trail. Future plans may include a connection across the river between these two trails in Massillon.

PARKING:
Parking is found along streets in Dalton, Sippo and in the two parks of Massillon.

A rest stop along the Sippo Valley Trail.

FOR MORE INFORMATION:

Rails-to-Trails of Wayne County
P.O. Box 1566, Wooster, OH 44691
Keith Workman, 330-682-7188

Village of Dalton
1 W. Main St., Dalton, OH 44618
330-828-2221

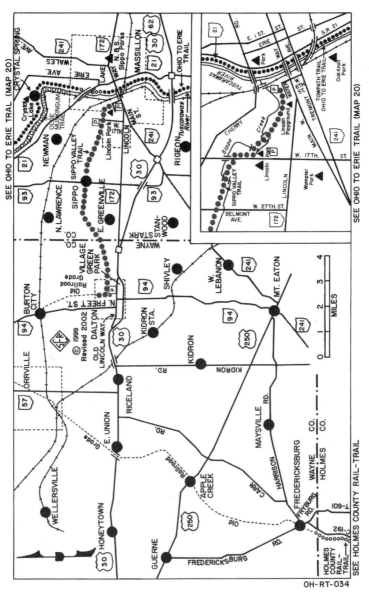

OH-RT-034

SIPPO VALLEY TRAIL
WAYNE & STARK COUNTIES
9.0   MILES
SURFACE: ASPHALT & SMOOTH
CRUSHED GRAVEL

HURON RIVER GREENWAY

VICINITY: *Huron*
TRAIL LENGTH: *12.8 Miles (Trail Incomplete)*
SURFACE: *Smooth Crushed Gravel*
TRAIL USE:

The Huron River Greenway has a very rich history of the earliest firelands to be settled. This includes Native American burial mounds and Fort Avery, which was used during the war of 1812. In 1827 the Milan Canal was built between Huron on Lake Erie and Milan; the canal operated from 1839 to 1869, until it was destroyed by a flood. In 1877, the Milan Canal was replaced by the Wheeling and Lake Erie Railway. By the 1990s, the railroad stopped operating, and the land was turned over to the Erie County Metroparks. Today, trail users can enjoy this beautiful trail with its rich history preserved.

From Huron, a signed bike route follows River Road between US Route-6 and the trail head parking area (south of State Route-2 overpass); both the foot nature trails and the rail-trail start here. From the trail head, the Huron River Greenway curves south through some woodlands, then across a spectacular wetland with plenty of wildlife to enjoy. From here, the trail continues south to Mason Road (this section will open in 2004). Plans are for the rest of the Huron River Greenway to continue south to Milan and Norwalk, where a connection with the North Coast Inland Bike Path will be made.

PARKING:
Parking is available in Huron on River Road and Mason Road.

An observation shelter makes wildlife viewing enjoyable.

FOR MORE INFORMATION:

Erie Metroparks
3910 E. Perkins Ave.,
Huron, OH 44839
419-625-7783

Huron River Greenway Coalition
632 River Rd., Huron, OH 44839
419-433-6180

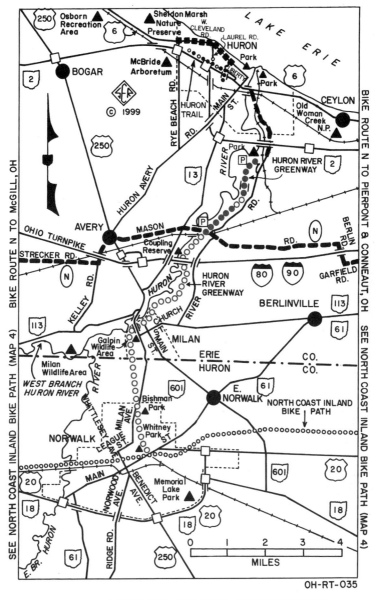

OH-RT-035

HURON RIVER GREENWAY
HURON & ERIE COUNTIES
12.8 MILES (TRAIL INCOMPLETE)
SURFACE: SMOOTH CRUSHED GRAVEL

CLINTON RAIL-TRAIL

VICINITY: *Wilmington*
TRAIL LENGTH: *1.5 Miles (Will be 30.0 Miles)*
SURFACE: *Asphalt*
TRAIL USE:

The Clinton Rail-Trail traverses 30 miles through Warren and Clinton Counties and connects to the 68-mile Little Miami Scenic Trail in Morrow. The trail starts in Morrow and goes northeast through Clarksville, Ogden, Wilmington, Melvin and Sabina. Between Morrow and Ogden, the Clinton Rail-Trail crosses Todd's Fork eight times as it winds through the hills of Southern Ohio. Between Clinton and Sabina, the rail-trail follows an existing railroad with a large separation of grass and trees.

Currently, most of this trail corridor is undeveloped, however, a 1.5-mile asphalt section of the Clinton Rail-Trail is open in Wilmington from Nelson Avenue to Mulberry Street. This short piece gives solitude to the bikers and walkers as they travel this quiet wooded section of the trail across town. In the future, other short sections of the Clinton Rail-Trail are expected to open.

PARKING:
Parking can be found along Mulberry Street in Wilmington.

The Clinton Rail-Trail winds through Wilmington.

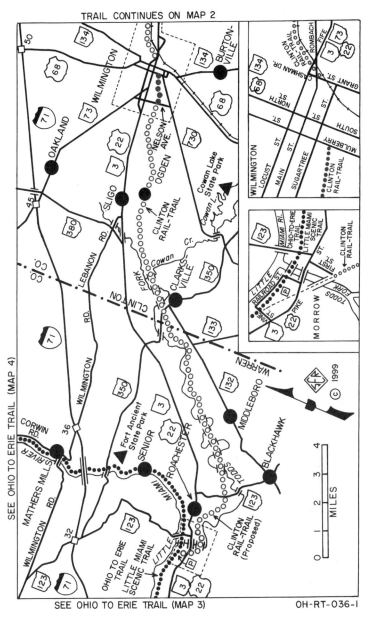

TRAIL CONTINUES ON MAP 2

SEE OHIO TO ERIE TRAIL (MAP 4)

SEE OHIO TO ERIE TRAIL (MAP 3)

OH-RT-036-I

© 1999

CLINTON RAIL-TRAIL (MAP 1)
WARREN & CLINTON COUNTIES
1.5 MILES
SURFACE: ASPHALT

Dean Focke gets ready to bike the Clinton Rail-Trail.

FOR MORE INFORMATION:

Clinton Rails-to-Trails Coalition
520 Dana Ave.,
Wilmington, OH 45177
937-382-3200

City of Wilmington
69 N. South St.,
Wilmington, OH 45177
937-382-4781

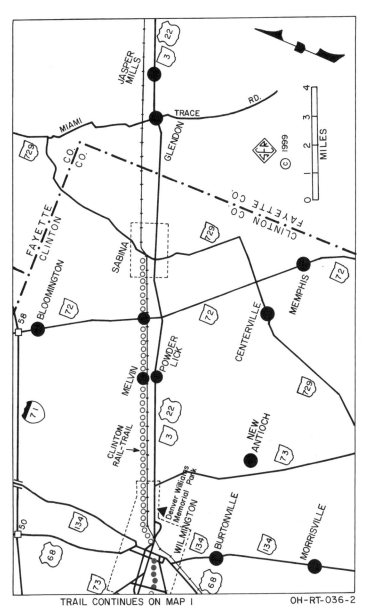

TRAIL CONTINUES ON MAP I

OH-RT-036-2

CLINTON RAIL-TRAIL (MAP 2)

BUCK CREEK BIKE PATH

VICINITY: *Springfield*
TRAIL LENGTH: *4.1 Miles*
SURFACE: *Asphalt*
TRAIL USE:

The Buck Creek Bike Path opened in 1998 and 1999 and follows Buck Creek through the center of Springfield from Plum Street to Pumphouse Road. Even though this trail follows a levee along Buck Creek, a small part does follow a former road and a former railroad between Limestone Street and Sherman Avenue. Attractions along the trail include Snyder Park, Wittenberg University, downtown Springfield, Lagonda Park, Old Reid Park and Buck Creek State Park. Although the Buck Creek Bike Path is 4.1 miles, it does connect to the 3-mile Northern Springfield Rail-Trail giving trail users a trail network of 7.1 miles.

If you take Fountain Avenue south from the Buck Creek Bike Path, then turn right on Jefferson Street, you will reach the north end of the 68-mile Little Miami Scenic Trail (Bike Route-1). In reverse from the Little Miami Scenic Trail, turn left on Center, then right on Columbia Street, then left on Fountain Avenue, and you will be back to the Buck Creek Bike Path.

PARKING:

Parking can be found in Buck Creek Park on Sherman Avenue and in Old Reid Park. You could also park in Buck Creek State Park.

Downtown Springfield.

FOR MORE INFORMATION:
National Trail, Parks & Recreation District
930 S. Tecumseh Road, Springfield, OH 45506
937-328-PARK (7275)

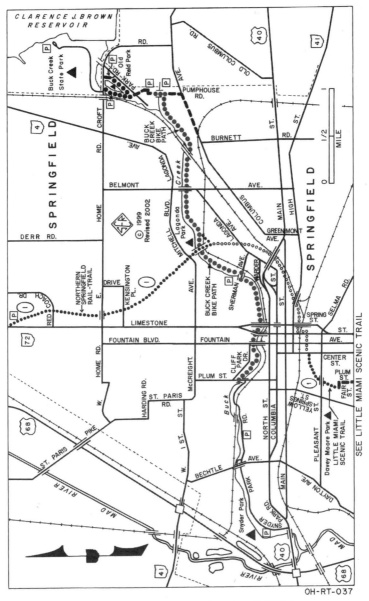

BUCK CREEK BIKE PATH
CLARK COUNTY
4.1 MILES
SURFACE: ASPHALT

TAYLORSVILLE METROPARK BIKE PATH (BIKE ROUTE-25)

VICINITY: *Dayton*
TRAIL LENGTH: *1.5 Miles*
SURFACE: *Asphalt*
TRAIL USE: 🚲 🛼 🚶 🏕️ 🐎 ⛷️ 🚶

The Taylorsville Metropark Bike Path is both a rail-trail and a former canal tow-path trail which is north of Dayton in Montgomery County. Highlights of this 1300-acre metropark are the wooded ravines, massive rock outcrops, the Great Miami River and the historical Miami & Erie Canal.

The trail starts in the northern part of Dayton along Rip Rap Road and goes north to US Route-40. From here, the trail goes north following the old Miami & Erie Canal. The trail's scenery mostly consists of bottom woodlands with plenty of wildlife. About one mile north is the site of the crossroads town of Tadmor, where at one time, the Old National Route (Old Route-40) and the Miami & Erie Canal intersected. This community also once had a railroad depot, a grain dealer's house, a house/store/post office building and a covered bridge. During the 1850s, this town was Montgomery County's busiest cross-roads. Today, very few remnants can be found. North of Tadmor, the asphalt trail ends. From this point on, only walkers can continue north of the metropark along the Miami & Erie Canal. Future plans for this bike path include making it part of the River Corridor Bikeway in Dayton.

PARKING:

Parking is found on Rip Rap Road and the northwest end of Taylorsville Dam along US Route-40.

The Taylorsville Metropark Bike Path.

FOR MORE INFORMATION:

Five Rivers Metroparks
1375 E. Siebenthaler Ave., Dayton, OH 45414
937-275-7275

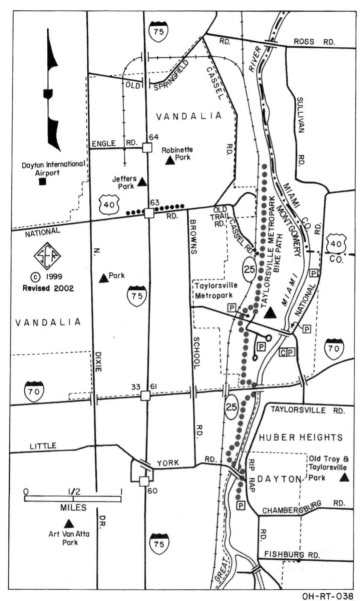

OH-RT-038

TAYLORSVILLE METROPARK BIKE PATH-25

MONTGOMERY COUNTY

1.5 MILES

SURFACE: ASPHALT

TOWNER'S WOODS RAIL-TRAIL

VICINITY: *Kent*
TRAIL LENGTH: *1.2 Miles*
SURFACE: *Smooth Crushed Gravel*
TRAIL USE: 🚲 🚵 🚶 ♿ 🐎 ⛷ 🚶

The Towner's Woods Rail-Trail is in the early stages of construction across Portage County from Kent to Ravenna. Currently, only 1.2 miles are open through Towner's Woods Park. This preserved greenway goes by woods, wetlands and remnant prairies; it also provides an excellent place for birdwatching. The major attraction along this trail is Towner's Woods Park, Portage County's oldest park. Hiking trails through Towner's Woods offer walkers a diversity of habitats.

Some day, the rail-trail may go as far east as Warren to connect with the Great Ohio Lake to River Greenway, and go west to connect with Kent and the Bike & Hike Trail system in Summit County.

PARKING:
Parking can be found in Towner's Woods Park on Ravenna Road.

Hikers can enjoy the Towner's Woods Rail-Trail.

FOR MORE INFORMATION:
Portage County Park District
449 Meridian St., Ravenna, OH 44266
330-673-9404

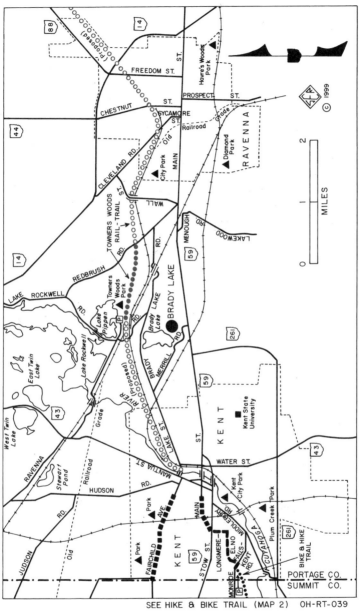

SEE HIKE & BIKE TRAIL (MAP 2)   OH-RT-039

TOWNERS WOODS RAIL-TRAIL
PORTAGE COUNTY
1.2   MILES
SURFACE: SMOOTH CRUSHED GRAVEL

GREAT OHIO LAKE TO RIVER GREENWAY

VICINITY: *Ashtabula/Warren/Youngstown/Lisbon*
TOTAL TRAIL LENGTH: *86 miles (Trail Incomplete)*
LOCAL SECTIONS & TRAIL LENGTHS:
(WESTERN RESERVE GREENWAY) *9.0 Miles; Ashtabula-Austinburg)*
(CANFIELD RAIL-TRAIL) *10.0 Miles; Canfield*
(LITTLE BEAVER CREEK GREENWAY TRAIL) *8.5 Miles; Leetonia-Lisbon*
SURFACE: *Asphalt*
TRAIL USE: 🚲 🚴 🧍 🏕️ 🐎 ⛷️ 🚶

The Great Ohio Lake to River Greenway will be a major cross-state trail through the far northeast section of Ohio. This trail starts on Lake Erie in Ashtabula and ends on the Ohio River in East Liverpool. This trail will be a rail-trail from Ashtabula to Lisbon, and a canal towpath trail from Lisbon to East Liverpool. When complete, this trail will go in a north-south direction through Ashtabula, Trumbull, Mahoning and Columbiana Counties. Near East Liverpool, the trail will be less than a mile from the state of Pennsylvania.

The Great Ohio Lake-to-River Greenway Coalition's vision is for the 85-mile greenway to pass through farm country, woodlands, rolling hills and along rivers, while at the same time preserving the heritage of the railroad and the canal. When complete, this trail "will provide transportation benefits and year-round recreational use for Northeast Ohioans for future generations to come."

The first two pioneer sections of the Great Ohio Lake to River Greenway opened in 2000. Under two different local trail names, the Canfield Rail-Trail and the Little Beaver Creek Greenway Trail are now open to trail users. The Canfield Rail-Trail goes 10.0 miles form Kirk Road, through the center of Canfield, to the Trumbull County Line. The Little Beaver Creek Greenway Trail follows the Middle Fork Little Beaver Creek for 8.5 miles from Leetonia on State Route-358 to Lisbon on State Route-164.

A third section of the trail opened in 2001 and is known as the Western Reserve Greenway. This trail starts on West Avenue in Ashtabula and goes 8.5 miles southwest to Austinburg; the trail ends one mile south of Austinburg on Lampson Road. Other sections of the Great Ohio Lake to River Greenway will open in the near future. For the latest information, contact the addresses on page 134.

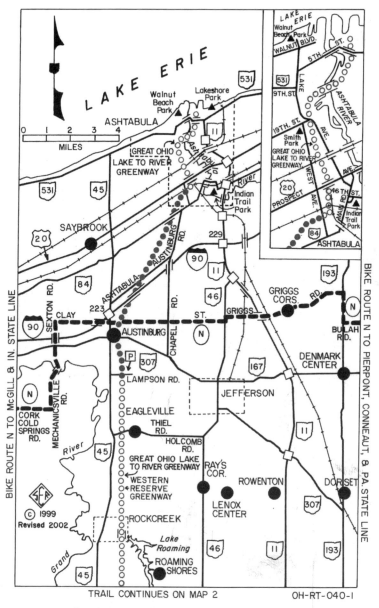

TRAIL CONTINUES ON MAP 2   OH-RT-040-1

GREAT OHIO LAKE TO RIVER GREENWAY (MAP 1)

ASHTABULA, TRUMBULL, MAHONING, & COLUMBIANA COUNTIES

5.7 & 8.5 MILES; SURFACE: ASPHALT

PARKING FOR WESTERN RESERVE GREENWAY:
Parking is found on Lampson Road south of Austinburg.

PARKING FOR CANFIELD RAIL-TRAIL:
Parking is found on the streets in Canfield.

PARKING FOR LITTLE BEAVER CREEK GREENWAY TRAIL:
Parking can be found on the streets in Leetonia as well as Coke Ovens Aboretum. Parking can also be found in Lisbon next to State Route-164 and two miles north of Lisbon on St. Jacob-Logtown Road.

The Great Ohio Lake to River Greenway spans over Rock Creek in Ashtabula County. (Photo by Kevin Grippi)

FOR MORE INFORMATION:

Ashtabula County:
Ashtabula Co. Parks
25 W. Jefferson St.,
Jefferson, OH 44047
440-576-0717

Western Reserve Greenway
134 W. 46th St.,
Ashtabula, OH 44004
440-992-8132

Trumbull County:
Trumbull County Metroparks
347 N. Park Avenue,
Warren, OH 44481
330-675-2480

Columbiana County:
Columbiana County Park District
130 W. Maple St., Lisbon, OH 44432
330-424-9078

Mahoning County:
Mahoning County
P.O. Box 596, Canfield, OH 44406
330-702-3000

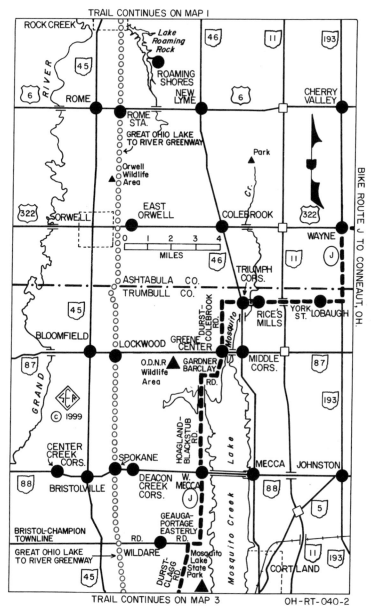

TRAIL CONTINUES ON MAP 1

ROCK CREEK

Lake Roaming Rock

46   11   193

45

RIVER

6   ROME

ROAMING SHORES

NEW LYME

6

CHERRY VALLEY

ROME STA.

GREAT OHIO LAKE TO RIVER GREENWAY

Park

Orwell Wildlife Area

322   SORWELL

EAST ORWELL

COLEBROOK

322   WAYNE

BIKE ROUTE J TO CONNEAUT, OH.

0 1 2 3 4
MILES

46

11   J

ASHTABULA   CO.
TRUMBULL   CO.

TRIUMPH CORS.

45

DURST-COLEBROOK RD.

RICE'S MILLS

YORK ST.   LOBAUGH

Mosquito

BLOOMFIELD

LOCKWOOD

GREENE CENTER

MIDDLE CORS.

87

GRAND

O.D.N.R Wildlife Area

GARDNER BARCLAY

87

193

RD.

© 1999

HOAGLAND-BLACKSTUB RD.

Lake

CENTER CREEK CORS.

SPOKANE

DEACON CREEK CORS.

W. MECCA
J

MECCA   JOHNSTON

88

BRISTOLVILLE

88

5

GEAUGA-PORTAGE EASTERLY RD.

Mosquito Creek

BRISTOL-CHAMPION TOWNLINE

RD.

GREAT OHIO LAKE TO RIVER GREENWAY

WILDARE

Mosquito Lake State Park

11   193

45

DURST-CLAGG RD.

CORTLAND

TRAIL CONTINUES ON MAP 3

OH-RT-040-2

GREAT OHIO LAKE TO RIVER GREENWAY (MAP 2)

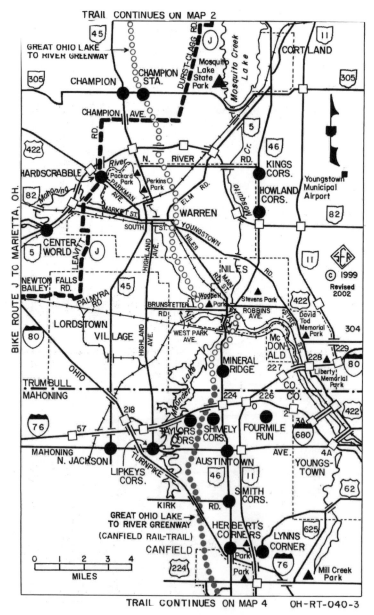

TRAIL CONTINUES ON MAP 2

GREAT OHIO LAKE
TO RIVER GREENWAY

45

305

CHAMPION

DURST-CLAGG RD.

J

CORTLAND

11

Mosquito Creek Lake

CHAMPION STA.

Mosquito Lake State Park

305

CHAMPION AVE.

422

RD.

N. RIVER RD.

5

46

KINGS CORS.

HARDSCRABBLE

River

Packard Park

PARKMAN AVE.

Perkins Park

82

Mahoning

MARKET ST.

ELM RD.

HOWLAND CORS.

Youngstown Municipal Airport

Mosquito Cr.

82

BIKE ROUTE J TO MARIETTA, OH.

SOUTH ST.

WARREN

YOUNGSTOWN

NILES

5

CENTER WORLD

J

LEAVITT

HIGHLAND AVE.

NILES RD.

MAIN ST.

RD.

11

SER

© 1999
Revised 2002

NEWTON FALLS BAILEY RD.

45

PALMYRA RD.

BRUNSTETTER RD.

Wadbet Park

WEST PARK AVE.

Stevens Park

ROBBINS AVE.

422

STATE

David Tod Memorial Park

304

LORDSTOWN VILLAGE

80

OHIO

HIGHLAND AVE.

Meander Lake

MINERAL RIDGE

McDONALD

227

228

229

Liberty Memorial Park

80

TRUMBULL
MAHONING

224

226

CO.
CO.

422

76

218

57

TAYLORS CORS.

SHIVELY CORS.

FOURMILE RUN

3A

680

MAHONING
N. JACKSON

TURNPIKE

LIPKEYS CORS.

AUSTINTOWN

46

11

AVE.

4A

YOUNGS-TOWN

62

KIRK RD.

SMITH CORS.

GREAT OHIO LAKE
TO RIVER GREENWAY
(CANFIELD RAIL-TRAIL)

HERBERT'S CORNERS

625

LYNNS CORNER

CANFIELD

224

Park

Park

76

Mill Creek Park

0   1   2   3   4
MILES

TRAIL CONTINUES ON MAP 4   OH-RT-040-3

3

GREAT OHIO LAKE TO RIVER
GREENWAY (MAP 3)

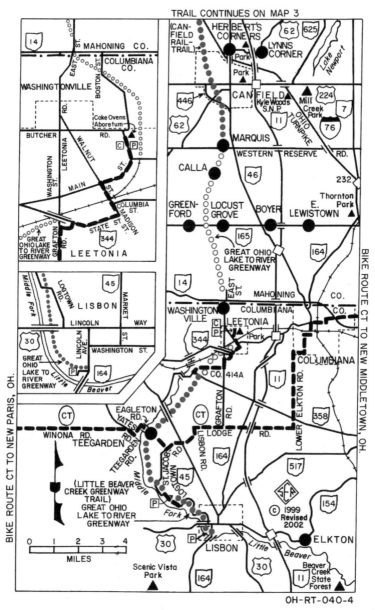

TRAIL CONTINUES ON MAP 3

OH-RT-040-4

GREAT OHIO LAKE TO RIVER GREENWAY (MAP 4)

OHIO'S MAJOR BIKE TRAILS

RIVER CORRIDOR BIKEWAY(BIKE ROUTE-25)

VICINITY: *Dayton (Great Miami River)*
TRAIL LENGTH: *25.0 Miles*
SURFACE: *Asphalt*
TRAIL USE: 🚲 🛼 🚶 ⛸ 🐎 ⛷ 🥾

The River Corridor Bikeway follows the Great Miami River and the Stillwater River, creating an excellent cycling alternative for Dayton-area commuters. The trail also provides trail users with a relaxing path to walk or bicycle with family and friends without the worry of city traffic. The bikeway traverses much of Montgomery County from south to north, as it passes through Miamisburg, West Carrollton, Moraine and Dayton.

Beginning at the Montgomery-Warren County Line off of Cincinnati Pike, the trail follows the Great Miami River Levee through Miamisburg, then parallels Dayton- Cincinnati Pike on its way to West Carrollton; an expanse of grass and trees keeps the bikeway and its users safely separated from the pike. The trail goes around the northwest side of West Carrollton. Traces of the old Miami & Erie Canal can be seen. It then goes to Marina Drive and out of West Carrollton. A two-mile segment of this section, with no roads in sight, abounds with scenery and serenity. Due to the lack of space for both a road and a bikeway, trail users must use the River Road for about one-half mile before the bikeway resumes to follow the Great Miami River around a bend to the town of Moraine and Old River Park on the south edge of Dayton.

The River Corridor Bikeway crosses a steel span bridge through Island Park.

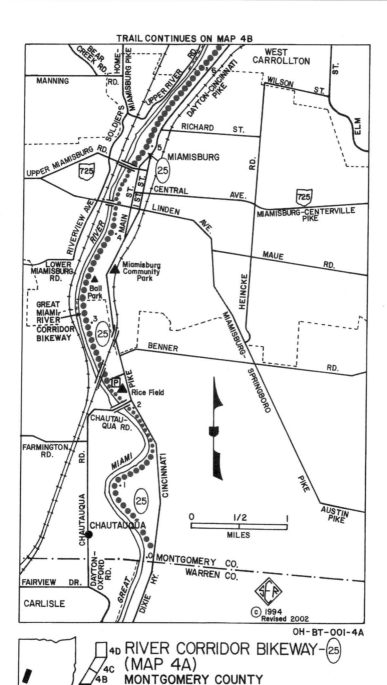

TRAIL CONTINUES ON MAP 4B

WEST CARROLLTON

MANNING

BEAR CREEK RD.
HOME-
MIAMISBURG PIKE
UPPER RIVER RD.
DAYTON-CINCINNATI PIKE
WILSON ST.
ST.
ELM

SOLDIERS
RD.
RICHARD ST.
ST.

UPPER MIAMISBURG RD.
725
5
MIAMISBURG
25
RD.

RIVERVIEW AVE.
RIVER
MAIN ST.
1ST ST.
CENTRAL AVE.
LINDEN AVE.
725
MIAMISBURG-CENTERVILLE PIKE

LOWER MIAMISBURG RD.
Miamisburg Community Park
Ball Park
MAUE RD.

GREAT MIAMI RIVER CORRIDOR BIKEWAY
3
25
HEINCKE
MIAMISBURG-SPRINGBORO

BENNER
RD.

IP
PIKE
Rice Field
2

CHAUTAU-QUA RD.

FARMINGTON RD.
RD.
MIAMI
CINCINNATI
1
25

CHAUTAUQUA
CHAUTAUQUA

PIKE
AUSTIN PIKE

0   1/2   1
MILES

MONTGOMERY CO.
WARREN CO.

FAIRVIEW DR.
DAYTON-OXFORD RD.
GREAT
DIXIE HY.
SFR
© 1994 Revised 2002

CARLISLE

OH-BT-001-4A

4D RIVER CORRIDOR BIKEWAY-25
4C (MAP 4A)
4B MONTGOMERY COUNTY
4A 25 MILES, SURFACE: ASPHALT

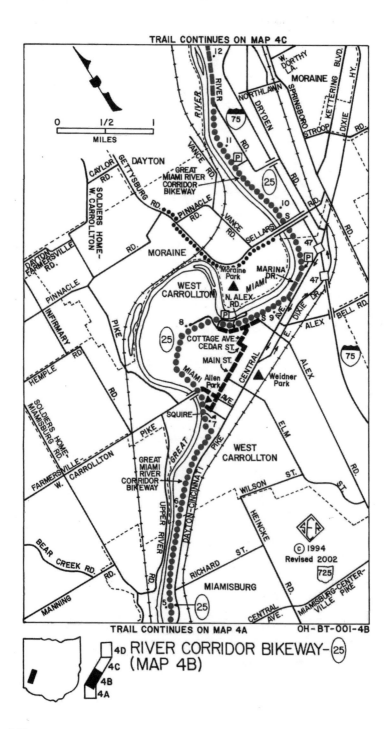

TRAIL CONTINUES ON MAP 4C

MORAINE

DAYTON

GREAT MIAMI RIVER CORRIDOR BIKEWAY

MORAINE

WEST CARROLLTON

Moraine Park

MARINA DR.

N. ALEX. RD.

COTTAGE AVE.
CEDAR ST.
MAIN ST.

Allen Park

Weidner Park

SQUIRE

WEST CARROLLTON

GREAT MIAMI RIVER CORRIDOR BIKEWAY

© 1994
Revised 2002

MIAMISBURG

TRAIL CONTINUES ON MAP 4A

OH-BT-001-4B

RIVER CORRIDOR BIKEWAY-②⑤
(MAP 4B)

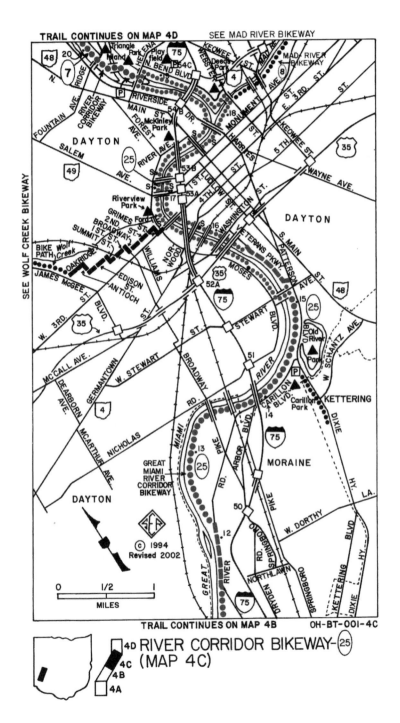

One mile up the trail from Old River Park, trail users encounter the Stewart Avenue Bridge, where the bikeway splits to run up both the east and west side of the river. While both sides of the trail offer a clear view of the bikeway on the opposite side, users that plan to connect with the Wolf Creek Bikeway should take the west side; users who plan to connect with the Mad River Bikeway should take the east side. There is limited access to both sides of the trail between Stewart Avenue and Helena Street and bicyclists will have to carry their transports up or down stairs; wheelchair users may want to avoid trying to enter or exit the trail at this point. The two trails join together at Helena Street and go north through Island Park where a span bridge takes users across the Stillwater River. The trail then follows the Stillwater River through Triangle and DeWeese parks in Dayton's north end. The trail ends at Shoup Mill Road.

Future plans for the River Corridor Bikeway include extending it in several directions. The bikeway will eventually follow the Great Miami River south through Warren, Butler and Hamilton Counties. Long-range plans will extend the trail northwest along Stillwater River to Troy and Piqua. A third extension may be made northward up the Great Miami River to Taylorsville Metropark. For current information, contact the address below.

PARKING:
Parking for this trail is available at Rice Field next to Cincinnati Pike just south of Miamisburg, along the streets of West Carrollton, at Carillon Park in Moraine along Carillon Boulevard, at Island Park in Dayton along Helena Street and at DeWeese Park in North Dayton along Siben-Thaler Avenue.

River Corridor Bikeway in downtown Dayton.

FOR MORE INFORMATION:
Miami Valley Regional Bicycle Council, Inc.
333 W. 1st St., Suite 150, Dayton, OH 45402
937-463-2707

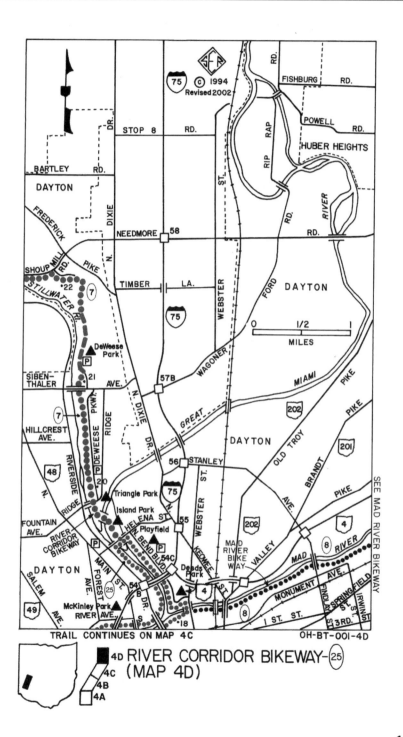

TRAIL CONTINUES ON MAP 4C   OH-BT-001-4D

4D **RIVER CORRIDOR BIKEWAY**-25
(MAP 4D)
4C
4B
4A

EMERALD NECKLACE TRAIL
VICINITY: *Cleveland*
TRAIL LENGTH: *69.0 Miles (Trail Incomplete)*
SURFACE: *Asphalt with Paralleling Dirt*
TRAIL USE:

INTERSTATE-480 BIKEWAY
VICINITY: *Cleveland*
TRAIL LENGTH: *3.0 Miles*
SURFACE: *Asphalt*
TRAIL USE:

ASPHALT SECTIONS COMPLETE FROM WEST TO EAST:

LOCATION	LANDMARKS	MILES
Lakewood-Middleburg Heights	Detroit Ave. to Bagley Rd.	13.5
Middleburg Heights-Strongsville	Bagley Rd. to W. 130th St.	8.0
Parma-Strongsville	Brookpark Rd. to Rocky R. Pkwy.	7.5
Brecksville Section	Brecksville Rd. to Towpath Trail	4.0
Walton Hills to Bedford	Alexander Rd. to Broadway	4.5
Bedford-Solon	Broadway to New Harper Rd.	6.0
Solon-Bentleyville	New Harper Rd. to Miles Rd.	3.5
Mayfield-Willoughby Hills	N. Chagrin Reservation to Chardon Rd.	4.0

TOTAL MILEAGE OPEN TO BICYCLISTS ON THE EMERALD NECKLACE TRAIL 51.0

The Emerald Necklace Trail winds through the Cleveland Metroparks, a series of reservations created by enthused Clevelanders in 1917 to preserve natural land for future generations. Today the Metroparks system consists of over 19,000 acres of land on 13 reservations. This beautiful park system provides Cleveland area residents with outdoor recreation, scenic nature preserves, picnic areas, sporting fields, wildlife management areas and waterfowl sanctuaries. The trail and park system offers bicycling, hiking, horseback riding, physical fitness trails, golf courses, swimming, boating and fishing, as well as sledding, skating and cross-country skiing during winter months. Six nature centers in the park system provide nature exhibits and other programs.

At this time, the Emerald Necklace Trail consists of eight separate stretches of paved bicycle paths and utilizes the Cross-State Bike Route-N to connect several of its sections through the south and southeast end of Cleveland. The six maps on the following pages show both the existing bike paths and the best suitable park roads to take trail users from one trail to another. A bridle path also parallels most of the paved bike paths, but equestrian enthusiasts should contact the Cleveland MetroParks System for detailed information.

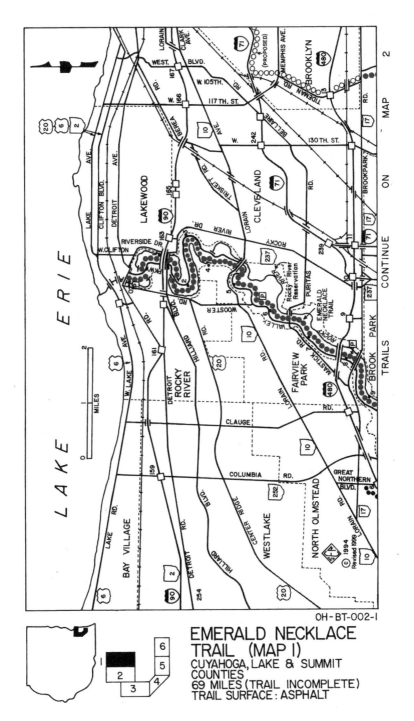

OH-BT-002-1

EMERALD NECKLACE TRAIL (MAP 1)
CUYAHOGA, LAKE & SUMMIT COUNTIES
69 MILES (TRAIL INCOMPLETE)
TRAIL SURFACE: ASPHALT

The west side of the Emerald Necklace Trail, along with the Interstate-480 Bikeway, offers users the best developed network of bike paths in Cleveland's west end. Several paved bike trails totaling 29 miles guide users through the Rocky River Reservation as well as in and out of Lakewood, Rocky River, Fairview Park, Brook Park, North Olmstead, Berea, Parma, Parma Heights, Middleburg Heights and Strongsville. This network of individual paths starts in Lakewood near Lake Erie on Cleveland's west side and goes south to Strongsville before turning southeast to West 130th Street where the western section ends.

The Emerald Necklace Trail near Lakewood.

A wooded section of the Emerald Necklace Trail.

From west 130th Street, trail users join the light traffic of spectacular Valley Parkway to Brecksville Road to access the south side of the Emerald Necklace Trail and four miles of the path's most scenic stretch. This section of trail intersects with the Towpath Trail in the Cuyahoga Valley National Recreation Area. To reach the Bedford Reservation, trail users take the Towpath Trail north to Tinkers Creek Road and follow the "Bike Route-N" signs to Dunham Road and Gorge Parkway. The parkway takes trail users through the Bedford Reservation where it joins a breathtaking 4.5-mile segment of the Emerald Necklace Trail that negotiates curves and hills and provides a good workout. This same section of path leads south to Alexander Road where it connects to the Bike and Hike Trail to Stow and Kent.

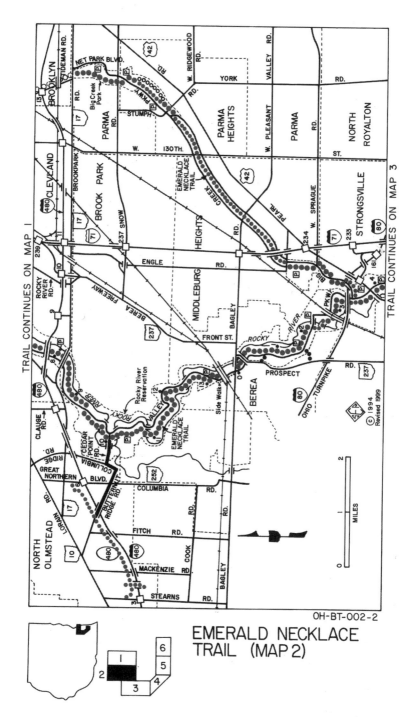

OH-BT-002-2

EMERALD NECKLACE
TRAIL (MAP 2)

Two sections of paved bike paths make up the southeastern and eastern portions of the Emerald Necklace Trail. From the Bedford Reservation in Walton Hills, the trail continues 9.5 miles northeast to the South Chagrin Reservation in Bentleyville, while a 4-mile network of paved trail runs near Mayfield and Willoughby in the North Chagrin Reservation. Trail users taking the Chagrin River Road between the South and North Chagrin Reservations should use caution; traffic on the road is often quite heavy.

Various extensions and connections are planned for the Emerald Necklace Trail. For current information, write to the addresses below.

PARKING:
Many parking areas are available all along the Emerald Necklace Trail.

The Emerald Necklace Trail between Bedford and Solon.

FOR MORE INFORMATION:

Emerald Necklace Trail
Cleveland Metroparks
4101 Fulton Parkway,
Cleveland OH 44144
216-351-6300

Interstate-480 Bikeway
City of North Olmsted
5200 Dover Center Rd., North
Olmsted, OH 44070
440-777-8000

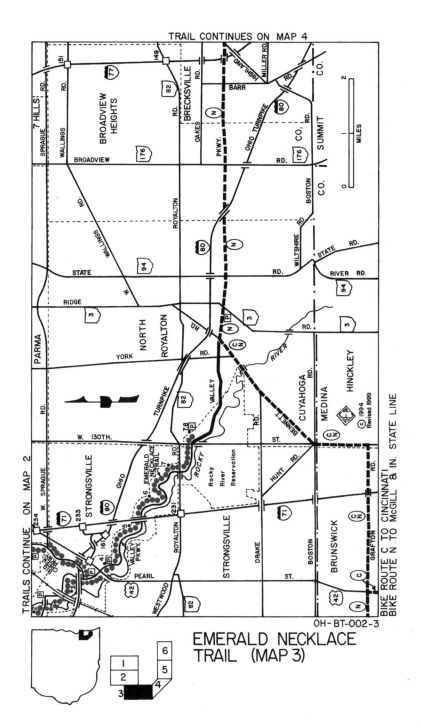

TRAIL CONTINUES ON MAP 4

EMERALD NECKLACE
TRAIL (MAP 3)

OH-BT-002-3

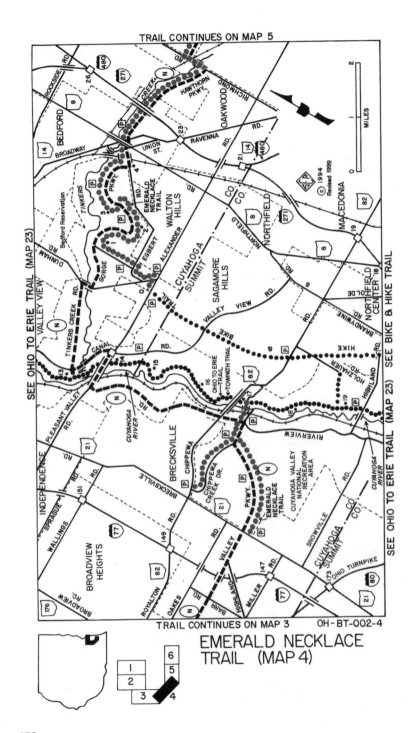

TRAIL CONTINUES ON MAP 5

OH-BT-002-4

EMERALD NECKLACE
TRAIL (MAP 4)

TRAIL CONTINUES ON MAP 3

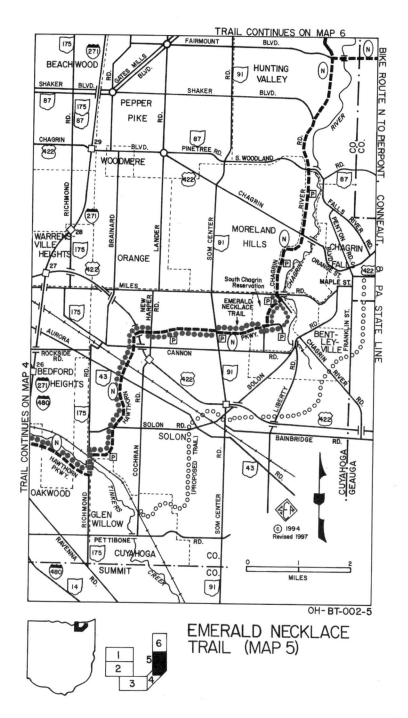

TRAIL CONTINUES ON MAP 6

EMERALD NECKLACE
TRAIL (MAP 5)

OH- BT-002-5

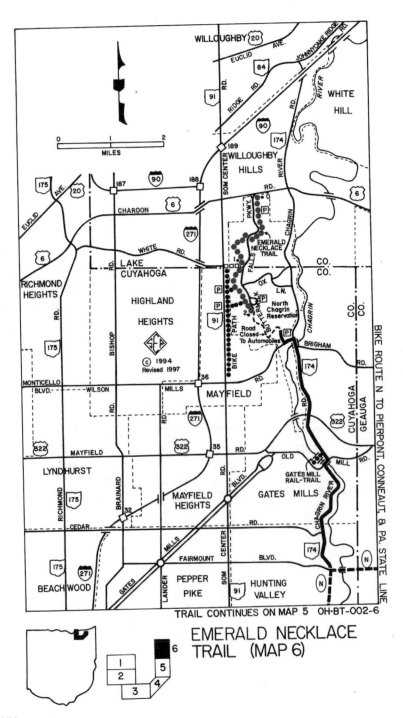

EMERALD NECKLACE
TRAIL (MAP 6)

TRAIL CONTINUES ON MAP 5   OH-BT-002-6

OHIO'S OTHER TRAILS & POTENTIAL RAIL-TRAILS

OHIO'S LIMITED USE RAIL-TRAILS

Limited Use Rail-Trails are extremely short in length and/or consist of a primitive (rough) surface. With either of these conditions, standard bicycle use may be prohibited, inappropriate, or very limited for most of these trails.

Please note that the (*) symbol indicates this minor rail-trail is shown on a map with a major featured rail-trail or bike trail.

CALIFORNIA JUNCTION TRAIL

VICINITY: *Hamilton County, in California, Ohio. Trail runs through the California Woods Nature Preserve near US Route-52.*
TRAIL LENGTH: *1.0 Mile*
SURFACE: *Dirt*
TRAIL USE:

CANAL LOCK TRAIL (*)

VICINITY: *Licking County, near Toboso, Ohio. Trail starts on north side of Licking River along Toboso Road in Blackhand Gorge. Keep in mind, certain sections of the trail including the tunnel are not part of the state property (See Ohio to Erie Trail, Map 15).*
TRAIL LENGTH: *2.0 Miles*
SURFACE: *Dirt and Gravel*
TRAIL USE:

DARKE COUNTY PARK DISTRICT TRAIL

VICINITY: *Darke County, in Greenville. Trail crosses over Greenville Creek between E. Water Street and North Broadway.*
TRAIL LENGTH: *0.5 Miles*
SURFACE: *Concrete*
TRAIL USE:

GATES MILLS TRAIL (*)

VICINITY: *Cuyahoga County, in Gatesmill. Trail follows Old Mill Road over the Chagrin River from Old Mill Road to Chagrin River Road (See Emerald Necklace Trail, Map 6).*
TRAIL LENGTH: *0.2 Miles*
SURFACE: *Asphalt*
TRAIL USE:

HURON TRAIL (*)

VICINITY: *Erie County, in Huron, Ohio. Trail follows US Route-6 through the northwestern end of Huron (See Huron River Greenway Map).*
TRAIL LENGTH: *1.5 Miles*
SURFACE: *Gravel*
TRAIL USE:

IRONTON RAIL-TRAIL

VICINITY: *Lawrence County, in Ironton. Trail goes from the intersection of Railroad and 8th Street to Ironton Hills Mall on US Route-52 and State Route- 93.*
TRAIL LENGTH: *0.3 Miles*
SURFACE: *Asphalt*
TRAIL USE:

KELLYS ISLAND RAIL-TRAIL

VICINITY: *Erie County, on Kelly's Island. The trail starts near the intersection of Division Street and Titus Road (State Route-575) next to the Glacial Grooves State Memorial. This rail-trail is part of the network of backwoods trails accessing scenic views of Lake Erie and Canada from the northwest portion of Kelly's Island.*
TRAIL LENGTH: *2.0 Miles*
SURFACE: *Gravel and Dirt*
TRAIL USE:

MARIETTA RAILROAD BRIDGE TRAIL

VICINITY: *Washington County, in Marietta. Over the Muskingum River right next to the Ohio River, this trail connects Maple Street to Butler Street in downtown Marietta.*
TRAIL LENGTH: *0.3 Miles*
SURFACE: *Concrete*
TRAIL USE:

TIFFIN RAIL-TRAIL

VICINITY: *Seneca County, in Tiffin. The narrow 3-foot wide asphalt trail is located in the Median of Benner Street; this section of trail goes from N. Washington Street to N. Sandusky Street (State Route-53). As a coarse gravel trail,it then goes from N. Sandusky Street to Hopewell Avenue and the Seneca County Fairgrounds.*
TRAIL LENGTH: *1.4 Miles*
SURFACE: *0.8 Miles Asphalt and 0.6 Miles Gravel*
TRAIL USE:

WELLSTON RAIL-TRAIL

VICINITY: *Jackson County, in Wellston. The trail parallels the east side of an active railroad through the center of Wellston from Second Street to State Routes-93 and 349. The trail then parallels State Route-349 northeast to Wellston's city limits.*
TRAIL LENGTH: *1.8 Miles*
SURFACE: *Asphalt, Smooth Crushed Gravel and Gravel*
TRAIL USE:

OHIO'S MINOR BIKE TRAILS

These minor bike trails consist of either an asphalt or a smooth crushed gravel surface. Many of these short trails parallel rivers, streams, highways, roads, or railroads. Others cover an area such as a park, or serve as a neighborhood connector. This list was compiled from various state, county and local government sources.

Please note that the (*) symbol indicates this bike path is shown on a map with a major featured bike trail or rail-trail.

ALLEN COUNTY
Bluffton	1.8 miles	Triplett Bike Path (Lake Rd. to Bluffton Village Park)
Lima	1.9 miles	Lima Bikeway
Lima	5.1 miles	Ottawa River Bikeway (Collet St. Recreation Area to Heritage Park)

BELMONT COUNTY
| St.Clairsville | 0.3 mile | Waterworks Road Bike Path |

BUTLER COUNTY
| Hamilton | 3.6 miles | Hamilton Bike Path (Downtown Paralleling the Great Miami River) |

CLARK COUNTY
| Springfield | 0.5 mile(*) | Old Reid Park Bike Path (See Buck Creek Bike Path) |

COSHOCTON COUNTY
| Coshocton | 3.0 miles(*) | Coshocton to Lake Park Bike Path (Trail mostly follows Walhonding River from Bridge St. to Lake Park) (See Ohio to Erie Trail, Map 17) |
| Coshocton | 1.2 miles(*) | Towpath Trail (Roscoe Village) (Whitewoman St. to Upper Basin) (See Ohio to Erie Trail, Map 17) |

CUYAHOGA COUNTY
Bay Village	1.0 mile	Huntington-Porter Creek Bike Trail
Cleveland	1.2 miles	Cleveland Lakefront State Park- Gordon Park Bike Trail (part of 10.1 mile bikeway from 9th St. to Euclid Beach Park)
Cleveland	0.5 mile	Edgewater Beach State Park Bike Trail
Cleveland Hts.	1.5 miles	Forest Hill/Cumberland/Cain Parks Bike Trail
Cleveland Hts.	2.0 miles	Shaker Lakes Parks Bike Trail
Euclid	2.5 miles	Euclid Creek Metropark Bike Trail (Euclid Creek Reservation)

Garfield Hts.	2.4 miles	Garfield Metropark Bike Trail (Garfield Park Reservation)
Mayfield Village	2.1 miles	State Route-91 Bike Route (Wilson Mills Rd. to Lake Cuyahoga County Line)
Newburgh Hts.	1.5 miles(*)	East 49th Street Bike Path (East 49th St. to Towpath Trail) (See Ohio to Erie Trail, Map 24)
Oakwood	1.6 miles	Forbes Road Bikeway

DELAWARE COUNTY

Powell	1.2 miles	Bennet Parkway Bike Path
Powell	1.0 mile	Liberty Street Bike Path
Powell	0.8 mile	Neighborhood North Park Bike Path (Liberty St.-Seldom Seen Rd.)
Powell	0.7 mile	Olentangy Street Bike Path (Consists of 3 segments of .3, .3 and .1 mile through Powell)
Powell	0.6 mile	Presidential Parkway Bike Path
Westerville	2.6 miles(*)	Cleveland Ave. Bike Path (See Westerville Bikeway)
Westerville	1.5 miles(*)	Polaris Parkway Bike Path (See Westerville Bikeway)
Westerville	1.0 mile(*)	Westerville Bikeway Parks & Playfield Loop Bike Paths (See Westerville Bikeway)

FRANKLIN COUNTY

Columbus	4.0 miles 3.0 miles 0.5 mile(*) 0.5 mile(*)	Alum Creek Bikeway (Williams Rd.-Watkins Rd.) (Wolfe Park) (Nelson Park) (See Ohio to Erie Trail, Map 10)
Columbus	0.5 mile(*)	Whetstone Park Bike Path (High St. to Olentangy/Lower Scioto Bikeways; see Olentangy/Lower Scioto Bikeways)
Columbus	0.3 mile(*)	Bike Route-2 (in Columbus) (Whetstone Park to Olentangy River Road; see Olentangy/LowerScioto Bikeways)
Columbus	0.5 mile(*)	Bike Route-5 (O.S.U.Campus Bike Path; see Olentangy/Lower Scioto Bikeways)
Dublin	1.7 miles	Avery Road Bike Path
Dublin	1.0 mile	Coffman Road Bike Path
Dublin	1.0 mile	Dublinshire Drive Bike Path

Dublin	1.0 mile	Earlington Parkway Bike Path
Dublin	1.5 miles	Emerald Parkway Bike Path (Coffman Rd. to State Route-257)
Dublin	1.0 mile	Emerald Parkway Bike Path (Rings Rd. to Innovation Drive)
Dublin	1.2 miles	Hard Road Bike Path
Dublin	1.7 miles	Muirfield Drive Bike Path
Dublin	2.5 miles	Paul G. Blazer Parkway Bike Path
Dublin	2.5 miles	Perimeter Drive Loop Road Bike Path
Dublin	1.0 mile	Sells Mill Drive Bike Path
Dublin	1.8 miles	South Fork Indian Run Bike Path
Dublin	1.5 miles	State Route-745 Bike Path
Dublin	1.5 miles	Tuller Road Bike Path
Dublin	0.7 mile	Village Pkwy.-Dublin Center Drive Bike Path
Dublin	1.5 miles	Wilcox Rd./Heather Glen Blvd. Bike Paths
Gahanna	2.2 miles 1.7 miles 0.5 mile	Blacklick Creek Bike Path(s) (Morse Rd.-Woodside Green Park) (Ridenour Rd.-Parkland Dr.)
Grove City	1.5 miles	Gantz Road Bike Path (Home Rd. to Ohio Dr.)
Hilliard	0.5 mile(*)	Avery Road Bike Path (See Ohio to Erie Trail, Map 8)
Hilliard	0.5 mile(*)	Britton Road Bike Path (See Ohio to Erie Trail, Map 8)
Hilliard	1.5 miles(*)	Davidson Road Bike Path (See Ohio to Erie Trail, Map 8)
Hilliard	1.0 mile (*)	Hilliard Municipal Park to Main Street Bike Path (See Ohio to Erie Trail, Map 8)
Hilliard	0.8 mile(*)	Homestead Park Bike Path (Cosgray Road and Heritage Rail-Trail) (See Ohio to Erie Trail, Map 8)
Reynoldsburg	2.1 miles	Blacklick Creek Bike Path (Kennedy Park-Huber Park)
Reynoldsburg	4.0 miles	Blacklick Woods Metropark Bike Path

Westerville	2.6 miles(*)	Cleveland Avenue Bike Path (See Westerville Bikeway)
Westerville	0.5 mile(*)	Hoover Dam Levee Bike Path (Sunbury Road and Hoover Reservoir Dam) (See Westerville Bikeway)
Westerville	0.2 mile(*)	Main Street Bike Path (Cleveland Ave. to Alum Creek Park; see Westerville Bikeway)
Westerville	4.0 miles(*)	Sharon Woods Metropark Bike Path (Bike Route-56) (See Westerville Bikeway)
Worthington	0.8 mile(*)	State Route-161 Bike Path (Olentangy River Rd. to Evening St.; See Olentangy/Lower Scioto Bikeways)

GREENE COUNTY

Beaver Creek	2.0 miles(*)	Dayton-Xenia Road Bike Path City (Hanes Rd. to Rotary Park; see Bike Route-2)
Beaver Creek	1.0 mile (*)	Kemp Road Bike Path City (N. Fairfield Rd. to Clubside Dr.; see Bike Route-2)
Beaver Creek	1.0 mile (*)	N. Fairfield Road Bike Path(s) City (follows both sides of N. Fairfield Rd. from Interstate-675 to Kemp Rd.; see Mad River Bikeway)
Xenia	0.5 miles(*)	Fairgrounds Bike Path (Bike Route-2 to Fairground Rd.; see Bike Route-2)

HAMILTON COUNTY

Cincinnati	1.5 miles(*)	Cincinnati Dunham Sport Complex Bike Path; (see Ohio to Erie Trail, Map 1)
Greenhills	3.0 miles	Winton Woods Metropark Bike Paths
Harrison	9.3 miles	Shaker Trace Trail(s) (Located in Miami Whitewater Forest)
	1.3 miles	(Inner Loop Trail)
	8.0 miles	(Outer Loop Trail)
Sharonville	2.6 miles	Sharon Woods Metropark Bike Paths

HANCOCK COUNTY

Findlay	0.7 mile	Heritage Trail

LAKE COUNTY

East Lake	1.6 miles	State Route-91 Bikeway (From Vokes Dr. to State Route-283)

Ohio's Minor Bike Trails

LICKING COUNTY

Newark	0.7 mile(*)	North Fork Licking River Bike Path (Everett Ave. to Manning St.; See Ohio to Erie Trail, Map 15)
Newark	3.6 miles(*)	O.S.U. Campus Area Bike Paths (These bike paths connect to Evans Bike Trail, also known as the Ohio to Erie Trail; See Ohio to Erie Trail, Map 14)

LOGAN COUNTY

Lakeview	2.5 miles	Indian Lake State Park Bike Path (Russels Point to Lakeview Harbor to Old Field Beach)

LORAIN COUNTY

Elyria	3.0 miles(*)	Black River Bridgeway Trail (Follows the Black River through Black River Reservation Metro Park; see North Coast Inland Bike Path, Map 5)

LUCAS COUNTY

Oregon	3.0 miles	Pearson Metropark Bike Path (Trail located on Starr Ave.)
Ottawa Hills	1.6 miles(*)	Wildwood Metropark Bike Path (See University-Parks Hike-Bike Trail)
Sylvania	3.0 miles	Erie Street Bikeway
Sylvania	6.1 miles / 3.4 miles / 2.7 miles	Secor Metroparks Bike Paths (3.4-mile path) (2.7-mile path)
Sylvania	2.0 miles(*)	Sylvania Ave. Bikeway (See University-Parks Hike-Bike Trail)
Toledo	3.0 miles(*)	Ottawa Park Bike Paths (See University-Parks Hike-Bike Trail)
Toledo	1.8 miles(*)	Parkside Blvd. Bike Path (See University-Parks Hike-Bike Trail)
Toledo	1.5 miles(*)	South Cove Blvd. Bike Path (See University-Parks Hike-Bike Trail)
Toledo	3.3 miles	Swan Creek Metropark Bike Path
Whitehouse	5.3 miles(*)	Oak Openings Metropark Bike Paths (See Wabash Cannonball Trail)

MAHONING COUNTY

Youngstown	2.0 miles	Mill Creek Metropark E. Golf Bike-Hike Trail (From Shields Rd. to Boardman Canfield Rd. [US Route-224])

MEDINA COUNTY

| Hinkley Lake | 3.0 miles | Hinkley Lake Bike Path |
| Wadsworth | 2.0 miles | Silver Creek Bike Path |

MIAMI COUNTY

| Troy | 1.2 miles | Troy Bike Path (follow levee) |

MONTGOMERY COUNTY

Dayton	0.6 miles(*)	Dixie Highway Bike Path (See River Corridor Bikeway)
Dayton	2.0 miles(*)	James McGee Blvd. Bike Path (See Wolf Creek Rail-Trail)
Germantown	1.2 miles	Germantown Bike Path
Moraine	1.5 miles	Moraine Bike Path (Follows Gettysburg Rd. and Sellersburg Rd.)

STARK COUNTY

| Louisville | 1.0 mile(*) | Metzger Park Bike Paths (Connects to the Nickelplate Trail; See Nickelplate Trail) |

SUMMITT COUNTY

Cuyahoga Falls	2.0 miles(*)	Cuyahoga Falls Parks Bike Path (Bike & Hike Trail to Water Works, Kennedy and Galt Parks; See Bike & Hike Trail)
New Boston	0.5 mile(*)	Stanford Road Bike Path (Stanford Rd. to Towpath Trail (See Ohio to Erie Trail, Map 23)
Northfield	0.5 mile(*)	Carriage Trail Bike Path Center (This trail connects Holzhauer Rd. and the Bike & Hike Trail to the Towpath Trail; See either the Bike & Hike Trail or the Ohio to Erie Trail, Map 23)
Stow	1.6 miles(*)	Silver Springs Park-Gram Road Bike Path (See Bike & Hike Trail)
Twinsburg	1.3 miles(*)	Center Valley Bikeway (See Bike & Hike Trail)

VINTON COUNTY

| Hamden | 1.0 mile | Lake Alma State Park Bike Path |

WILLIAMS COUNTY

| Bryan | 0.6 mile | Moore Park Bike Path |

OHIO'S POTENTIAL RAIL-TRAILS

Ohio's Potential Rail-Trails

PROPOSED TRAIL NAME	MILES	END POINTS OF TRAIL
A.C. & Y. Trail	27	Delphos to Bluffton
Allen-Hardin-Marion Rail-Trail	46	Marion to Kenton to Lima
Alum Creek Multi-Use Trail	18	Columbus to Westerville
Athens to Belpre Trail	34	Athens to Belpre
Athens to Zaleski	18	Athens to Zaleski
Blanchard River Greenway	1	Findlay
C D + M Trail	9	Marion to Prospect
Cincinnati Riverfront Trail	11	Cincinnati; Downtown Area to Lunken Airport
Cinncinnati-Newport Bridge Trail	1	Cincinnati, OH to Newport, KY
Conotton Creek Trail	11	Bowerston to Jewett
Englewood Trail	3	Englewood
Evans Bike Trail (Extension)	12	Centerburg to Johnstown
Fairfield County Heritage Trail	20	Bremen to Stoutsville
Great Miami Path	30	Hamilton to Miamisburg
Great Ohio Lake to River Greenway	85	Ashtabula to E. Liverpool
Heart of Ohio Trail	117	Mansfield to Mt. Vernon to Millersburg to Orville to Massillon
Heise Park Trail	1	Galion
Iron Furnace Rail-Trail	6	Ironton to Vesuvius
Lake County Metroparks Trail	5	Painesville; Fairport Harbor to Lake-Geauga County Line
Madeira-Loveland Trail	6	Maderia to Loveland
Mansfield Historic Trail	10	Mansfield to Ashland County Line
Maple Highlands Trail	14	Chardon to Middlefield
Marietta Bike Trail	6	Marietta to SR-821
Mill Creek Greenway	28	Cincinnati to Hamilton
Nelsonville-Shawnee Bikeway	19	Nelsonville to Shawnee
North Coast Inland Trail	49	Toledo to Elyria

Northern Springfield Rail-Trail	6	Springfield to Champaign-Clark County Line
Ohio River Trail	14	Cincinnati to New Richmond
Ohio to Erie Trail	335	Cincinnati to Columbus to Cleveland
Perry County Trail	31	Thornville to Shawnee
Piqua Multi-Use Trail	6	Piqua
SWOTA Trail	7	Valley Junction to Harrison (Ohio to Indiana State Line)
Sardinia-Hillsboro Trail	20	Sardinia to Hillsboro
Simon Kenton Rail-Trail	10	Urbana to Champaign to Clark County Line
Solon-Chagrin Falls Trail	5	Solon to Chagrin Falls
Towpath Trail	87	Cleveland to Akron to Massillon (Ohio & Erie Canal) to Zoarville
Towner's Woods Rail-Trail	29	Kent to Warren
Westerville-Mt. Vernon Trail	35	Westerville to Mt. Vernon

For more information on receiving the developments of each trail, contact either of the addresses below: Ohio Field Office of the Rails-to-Trails Conservancy, 4930 Cherry Bottom Rd., Gahanna, OH 43230 or call 614-428-4320. Rails-to-Trails Conservancy, 1100 17th St. NW, 10th Floor, Washington, D.C. or call 202-331-9696.

FURTHER
BICYCLE
ROUTE
INFORMATION

COLUMBUS OUTDOOR PURSUITS

BIKE ROUTE MAPS

The bike maps listed below have been produced by the Columbus Outdoor Pursuits, a recreational club in Central Ohio. To order maps, contact the Columbus Outdoor Pursuits for the current prices. Next, photocopy this page, complete this form, then enclose a check for the appropriate amount made out to the Columbus Outdoor Pursuits, and mail it to: Columbus Outdoor Pursuits, P.O. Box 14384, Columbus, OH 43214 (614-447-1006). Make sure to include your name, address and telephone number.

http://www.webmaster@outdoor-pursuits.org

	ROUTE MAP	LENGTH	DESCRIPTION
___	Bike Route A	247 miles	Elizabethtown-Toledo
___	Bike Route B	240 miles	Cincinnati-Marietta
___	Bike Route C	283 miles	Cincinnati-Cleveland
___	Cardinal Trail Bike Route	313 miles	New Paris-Petersburg
___	Bike Route E	253 miles	Portsmouth-Toledo
___	Bike Route F	301 miles	New Paris-Dilles Bottom
___	Bike Route J	246 miles	Marietta-Conneaut
___	Bike Route K	164 miles	Payne-Mifflin
___	Bike Route N	311 miles	McGill-Pierpont and Conneaut

OTHER MAPS BY THE COLUMBUS OUTDOOR PURSUITS

___ "Biking Ohio's Rail-Trails" by Shawn E. Richardson

(Paperback book including information, maps and photographs of Ohio's rail-trails and bike trails.)

___ "Ed Honton takes you Cycling Through Central Ohio"

(A book of 43 day rides along Central Ohio's scenic back roads and rail- trails.)

___ "Columbus, Ohio & Franklin County Bicycle Route Guide"

(A folding multicolor map showing back roads, bike routes, bike lanes and bike paths.)

___ Total Cost of Maps Ordered (amount enclosed)

OHIO MAP-COLUMBUS OUTDOOR PURSUITS MAP

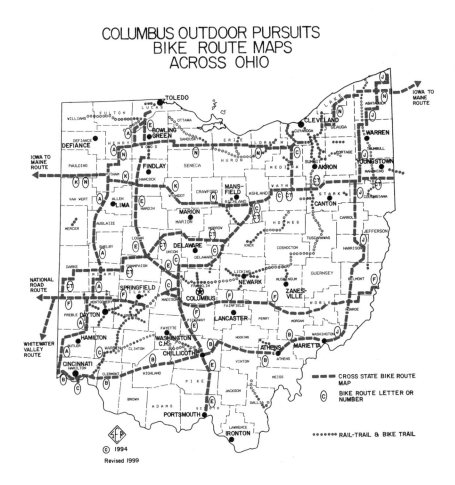

COLUMBUS OUTDOOR PURSUITS
BIKE ROUTE MAPS
ACROSS OHIO

© 1994
Revised 1999

OHIO'S PUBLISHED BICYCLE MAPS

OHIO (STATEWIDE COVERAGE)
"Biking Ohio Map & List of Bikeways in Ohio" Ohio Department of Transportation, Division of Multi Modal Planning and Programs, Bicycle/Pedestrian Program, P.O. Box 899, Columbus, OH 43216-0899
614-644-7095   Scale: 1 in.=24 miles.

A. FRANKLIN COUNTY (COLUMBUS)
"Columbus, Ohio & Franklin County Bicycle Route Guide" Columbus Outdoor Pursuits, P.O. Box 14384, Columbus, OH 43214.
614-447-1006   Scale: 1 in.=1.5 miles

B. HAMILTON, BUTLER, CLERMONT AND WARREN COUNTIES
"OKI-Bike Route Guides for Butler, Clermont, Hamilton, & Warren Counties." OKI-Regional Council of Governments, 801-B, W. 8th St., Suite 400, Cincinnati, OH 45203
513-621-7060   Set of 4 maps; Scale: 1 in.=2 miles

B. HAMILTON COUNTY (CINCINNATI)
"Cincinnati Bike Route Guide" OKI-Regional Council of Governments, 801-B, W. 8th St., Suite 400, Cincinnati, OH 45203.
513-621-7060   Scale: 1.9 in.=1 mile

C. HANCOCK COUNTY (FINDLAY)
"Findlay & Hancock County Bike Route System" Hancock County Park District, 819 Park St., 1833 Courthouse, Findlay, OH 45480.
419-423-6952   Scale: 1 in.=2 miles

D. LICKING COUNTY (NEWARK)
"Licking County Bicycle & Pedestrian Transportation Corridor Map", Thomas J. Evans Foundation, P.O. Box 4217, Newark, OH 43058.
740-349-8276   Scale: 1 in.=0.85 miles and 1 in.=0.27 miles

E. MONTGOMERY COUNTY (DAYTON)
"Metro Dayton By Bicycle," Miami Valley Regional Bicycle Council, Inc. 333 W. 1st St., Suite 150, Dayton, OH 45402.
937-463-2707   A set of 8 maps; Scale: 2.6 in.=1 mile

F. "IOWA TO MAINE ROUTE (#BC-110)"
Muscatine, IA to Bar Harbor, ME (1615 miles) map (#BC-1102, Section 2, for Ohio Only) Adventure Cycling Association (formerly Bike Centennial) P.O. Box 8308, Missoula, MT 59807-8308. 800-721-8719. A set of 4 maps for Iowa to Maine (One map for across Ohio Only).   Scale: 1 in.=4 miles

G. GREENE COUNTY (XENIA)
"Greene County, Greene Ways County-Wide Trails Map" Greene County Park District 651 Dayton-Xenia Rd., Xenia, OH 45385
937-376-7440   Scale: 1 in.=2 miles

H. CUYAGOGA, GEAUGA, LAKE, LORAIN & MEDINA COUNTIES
"Bicycle Transportation Map" County Series
Northeast Ohio Areawide Coordinating Agency, 216-241-2414, Ext. 273,
http://www.noaca.org   Scale: 1.25 in.=1 mile

YOUTH HOSTELS (U.S.A. & CANADA)
"Hosteling North America" Guidebook
American Youth Hostels (Hosteling International)
733 15th St. NW, Suite 480, Washington, DC 20005
202-783-6161

Additional Youth Hostels
The Hostel Handbook
"The Hostel Handbook for the U.S.A. & Canada"
722 St. Nicholas Ave., New York, NY 10031
212-926-7030

Note: For current prices, contact the appropriate offices. Readers can obtain a
free Ohio highway map by writing to the Ohio Department of Transportation,
1980 W. Broad St., Columbus, OH 43223 or by calling 614-466-7170

PUBLISHED BICYCLE MAPS
IN OHIO

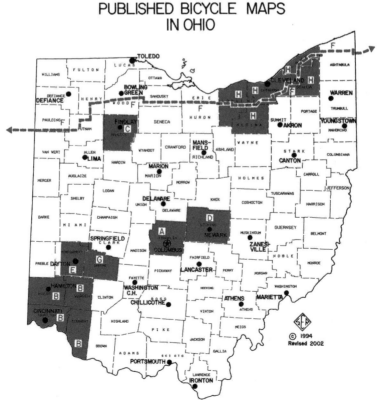

U.S. RAILS-TO-TRAILS GUIDE BOOKS

U.S. GENERAL
Biking USA'S Rail-Trails, Shawn E. Richardson, 2002, Adventure Publications, Inc., 820 Cleveland St. S, Cambridge, MN 55008, 800-678-7006. Trail Listings & Trail Location Maps Included for all 50 States.

CALIFORNIA
Rail-Trail Guide to California, Fred Wert, 1995, Infinity Press, P.O. Box 17883, Seattle, WA 98107. Maps Included.

The Official Rails-to-Trails Conservancy Guidebook, California, Tracy Salcedo-Chourre, 2001, The Globe Pequot Press, P.O. Box 480, Guilford, CT 06437. Maps Included.

FLORIDA
Florida's Paved Bike Trails, Jeff Kunerth & Gretchen Kunerth, 2001, University Press of Florida, 15 NW 15th St. Gainesville, FL 32611, http://www.upf.com. Maps Included.

The Official Rails-to-Trails Conservancy Guidebook, Florida, David Gluckman, 2001, The Globe Pequot Press, P.O. Box 480, Guilford, CT 06437. Maps Included.

ILLINOIS
Bicycle Trails of Illinois, 1996, American Bike Trails, 610 Hillside Ave., Antioch, IL 60002, 800-246-4627, http://www.abtrails.com. Maps Included.

IOWA
Bicycle Trails of Iowa, 1996, American Bike Trails, 610 Hillside Ave., Antioch, IL 60002, 800-246-4627, http://www.abtrails.com. Maps Included.

MASSACHUSETTS
Bike Paths of Massachusetts, Stuart Johnstone, 1996, Active Publications, P.O. Box 716, Carlisle, MA 01741. Maps Included.

MINNESOTA
Biking in Vikingland, Marlys Mickelson, 1999, Adventure Publications, Inc., 820 Cleveland St. S, Cambridge, MN 55008, 800-678-7006. Maps Included; book also shows some trails in Wisconsin.

MISSOURI
Biking Missouri's Rail-Trails, Shawn E. Richardson, 1999, Adventure Publications, Inc., 820 Cleveland St. S, Cambridge, MN 55008, 800-678-7006. Maps Included.

NEW JERSEY
24 Great Rail-Trails of New Jersey, Craig Della Penna, 1999, New England Cartographics Inc., P.O. Box 9369, North Amherst, MA 01059, 888-995-6277 OR 413-549-4124. Maps Included.

NEW YORK
Cycling along the Canals of New York, Louis Russi, 1999, Vitesse Press, 4431 Lehigh Rd., #288, College Park, MD 20740, 301-772-5915., http://www.acorn-pub.com. Maps Included.

OHIO

Biking Ohio's Rail-Trails, Shawn E. Richardson, 2002, Adventure Publications, Inc., 820 Cleveland St. S, Cambridge, MN 55008, 800-678-7006. Maps Included.

OREGON

The Official Rails-to-Trails Conservancy Guidebook, Washington & Oregon, Mia Barbera, 2001, The Globe Pequot Press, P.O. Box 480, Guilford, CT 06437. Maps Included.

PENNSYLVANIA

Pennsylvania's Great Rail-Trails, Rails-to-Trails Conservancy, 1998, RTC, 1100 17th. St. NW, 10th Floor, Washington, D.C. 20036, 202-331-9696. Maps Included.

Free Wheeling Easy in and Around Western Pennsylvania, Mary Shaw & Roy Weil, Associates, 414 S Craig St., #307, Pittsburgh, PA 15213, http://www.spoke.compose.ce.cmu.edu/fwe/fwe.htm. Maps Included.

WASHINGTON STATE

Washington's Rail-Trails, Fred Wert, 2001, The Mountaineers, 1011 SW Klickitat Way, Seattle, WA 98134, 800-553-4453, http://www.mountaineers.org. Maps Included.

The Official Rails-to-Trails Conservancy Guidebook, Washington & Oregon, Mia Barbera, 2001, The Globe Pequot Press, P.O. Box 480, Guilford, CT 06437. Maps Included.

WEST VIRGINIA

Adventure Guide to West Virginia's Rail-Trails, 1995, West Virginia Rails-to-Trails Council, P.O. Box 8889, South Charleston, WV 25303, 304-722-6558. Maps Included.

WISCONSIN

Biking Wisconsin's Rail-Trails, Shawn E. Richardson, 2003, Adventure Publications, Inc., 820 Cleveland St. S, Cambridge, MN 55008, 800-678-7006. Maps Included.

ATLANTIC STATES (DE, MD, VA, WV)

The Official Rails-to-Trails Conservancy Guidebook, MD, DE, VA, WV, Barbara A. Noe, 2000, The Globe Pequot Press, P.O. Box 480, Guilford, CT 06437. Maps Included.

NEW ENGLAND STATES (CT, MA, ME, NH, RI & VT)

Great Rail-Trails of the Northeast, Craig Della Penna, 1995, New England Cartographics Inc., P.O. Box 9369, North Amherst, MA 01059, 888-995-6277 or 413-549-4124. Maps Included.

The Official Rails-to-Trails Conservancy Guidebook, CT, RI, MA, VT, NH, ME Cynthia Mascott, 2000, The Globe Pequot Press, P.O. Box 480,Guilford, CT 06437. Maps Included.

OHIO'S TRAILS INDEX AND ADDRESSES

Ohio's Trails Index and Addresses

TRAILS INDEX AND WEB PAGES
RAIL-TRAIL & BIKE TRAIL WEB PAGES

BIKE & HIKE TRAIL
http://www.neo.rr.com/MetroParks/bh_main.html

CELINA-COLDWATER BIKEWAY
http://www.bright.net/~dietsch/grandlake/biketrail.htm

GALLIPOLIS BIKE PATH (GALLIA COUNTY HIKE & BIKE TRAIL)
http://www.eurekanet.com/~ovvc/biketrail.html

HOCKHOCKING-ADENA BIKEWAY
http://www.seorf.ohiou.edu/~xx088/

HURON RIVER GREENWAY
http://www.ourworld.compuserve.com/homepages/HRGC/homepage.htm
http://www.eriemetroparks.com

KOKOSING GAP TRAIL
http://www.railtrails.org/kokosinggap/

LESTER RAIL-TRAIL
http://www.medinacountyparks.com

LITTLE MIAMI SCENIC TRAIL
http://www.dnr.state.oh.us/odnr/parks/directory/lilmiami.htm
http://www.intellweb.com/trails/lmiami.htm
http://www.bright.net/~dietsch/biketrails/cincinnati.htm
http://www.yellowsprings.com/bikepath.html

NORTH COAST INLAND TRAIL
http://www.clydeohio.org/trail.htm
http://www.scpd-parks.org/ncit.html

TOWPATH TRAIL (OHIO & ERIE CANAL)
http://www.nps.gov/cuva/ohioerie.htm
http://www.starkparks.com/Default.htm

OHIO TO ERIE TRAIL
http://www.ohio-to-erie-trail.org

RICHLAND B. & O. TRAIL
http://www.virtualmansfield.com/bno-bike-trail.htm

TRI-COUNTY TRIANGLE TRAIL
http://www.members.tripod.com/tricotrail/

WABASH CANNONBALL TRAIL
http://www.toltbbs.com/~norta/

WESTERN RESERVE GREENWAY
http://www.interlaced.net./ashparks/flra.htm

WOLF CREEK RAIL-TRAIL
http://www.whizlinc.com/2000/wolfcreektrail/trailwelcome.htm

OTHER STATEWIDE GROUPS & REGIONS INVOLVED WITH RAIL-TRAILS

ADVENTURE CYCLING (FORMERLY BIKECENTENNIAL)
http://www.adv-cycling.org

BIKE MIAMI VALLEY
http://www.bikemiamivalley.org/

BIKING USA'S RAIL-TRAILS
http://www.BikingUSARailTrails.com

COLUMBUS OUTDOOR PURSUITS
http://www.webmaster@outdoor-pursuits.org

CYCLING OHIO TRAILS & BIKEWAYS
http://www.richnet.net/~bikeohio/

METROPARKS OF THE TOLEDO AREA (METROPARKS TRAILS)
http://www.metroparkstoledo.com/trails.html

MIAMI VALLEY, OHIO RAILS TO TRAILS
http://www.intellweb.com/trails/hotlist.htm

OHIO BICYCLE TRAILS: A BIKE TRAILS DIRECTORY
http://www.bright.net/~dietsch/biketrails/index.htm

OHIO DEPARTMENT OF TRANSPORTATION
http://www.dot.state.oh.us/bike/

RAILS TO TRAILS CONSERVANCY
http://www.railtrails.org

RAILS TO TRAILS CONSERVANCY, OHIO FIELD OFFICE
http://www.railtrails.org/OH

RAILS TO TRAILS PAGES HOT LIST OF LINKS
http://www.intellweb.com/trails/hotlist.htm

TRI-STATE BICYCLE FACILITIES
http://www.oki.org/bike.html

OHIO'S CHAMBER OF COMMERCE

Akron	.330-376-5550
Ashtabula	.440-998-6998
Athens	.740-594-2251
Barberton	.330-745-3141
Beavercreek	.937-426-2202
Bedford	.440-232-0115
Bedford Heights	.440-232-3369
Bellevue	.419-483-2182
Bellville	.419-886-2245
Berea	.440-243-8415
Bexley	.614-235-8694
Bowling Green	.419-353-7945
Brecksville	.440-526-7350
Broadview Heights	.440-838-4510
Brookville	.937-833-2375
Buckeye Lake	.740-929-2701
Canal Fulton	.330-854-2805
Celina	.419-586-2219
Chillicothe	.740-702-2722
Cincinnati (Greater)	.513-579-3100
Cincinnati (Anderson)	.513-474-4802
Cincinnati (Clermont Co.)	.513-753-7141
Cincinnati (Hamilton Co.)	.513-984-6555
Cincinnati (Over the Rhine)	.513-241-2690
Cleveland	.216-621-3300 and 888-304-4769
Cleveland Heights	.216-397-7322
Coldwater	.419-678-4881
Columbus	.614-221-1321
Coshocton	.740-622-5411
Cuyahoga Falls	.330-929-6756
Dalton	.330-828-2444
Dayton	.937-226-1444
Elyria	.(See Lorain)
Fairborn	.937-878-3191 and 937-878-0205
Fremont	.419-332-1591
Gahanna	.614-471-0451

Gallipolis 740-446-0596

Garfield Heights 216-475-7775

Garrettsville 330-527-2411

Grand Rapids 419-832-1106

Greenville 937-548-2102

Hilliard 614-876-7666

Huber Heights 937-233-5700

Hudson 330-650-0621

Huron 419-433-5700

Independence 216-573-2707

Ironton . . . .(See South Point)

Jamestown 937-675-5311

Johnstown 740-967-2334

Kelleys Island 419-746-2360

Kent 330-673-9855

Kent (Brimfield Area) 330-673-4919

Kettering 937-299-3852

Lakewood 216-226-2900

Lexington . . . .(See Mansfield)

Lisbon 330-424-1803

London 740-852-2250

Lorain . . . . .440-233-6500 and 440-323-9424

Louisville 330-875-7371

Loveland 513-683-1544

Mansfield 419-522-3211

Marietta 740-373-5176

Massillon 330-833-3146

Maumee 419-893-5805

Medina 330-723-8773

Miami Township . . . .(See Milford)

Miamisburg . . . .(See South Metro Dayton)

Middleburg Heights 440-243-5599

Milan . . . . .P.O. Box 544, Milan, OH 44846

Milford 513-831-2411

Millersburg 330-674-3975

Montpelier 419-485-4416

Moraine . . . .(See Kettering)

Morrow . . . . .513-899-4466 and 513-899-3366
Morrow (South Lebanon Area) 513-932-7185
Mount Vernon 740-393-1111
Munroe Falls . . . .(See Stow)
Nelsonville 740-753-4346
New Philadelphia 330-343-4474
Newark 740-345-9757
Niles . . . .(See Youngstown or Warren)
North Baltimore . . . . .419-257-3523 and 419-257-3514
North Royalton 440-237-6180
Northfield 330-467-8956
Norwalk 419-668-4155
Oakwood . . . .(See Kettering)
Oberlin . . . . .440-774-6262 and 800-962-3754
Orwell 440-437-6133
Parma 440-886-1700
Parma Heights . . . .(See Parma)
Pataskala .740-964-5503 and 740-964-6100
Ravenna 330-296-3886
Reynoldsburg 614-866-4753
Rock Creek 440-563-3340
Rocky River 440-331-1140
Saint Clairsville 740-695-9623
Saint Marys 419-394-4611
Solon 440-248-5080
South Metro Dayton 937-433-2032
South Point . . . . .740-377-4550 and 800-408-1334
Spring Valley 937-862-4110
Springfield 937-325-7621
Stow 330-688-1579
Strongsville 440-238-3366
Sylvania 419-882-2135
Tiffin 419-447-4141
Toledo . . . . .419-243-8191 and 419-242-6237
Trotwood 937-837-1484
Twinsburg 330-963-6249
Upper Arlington 614-481-5710

The tracks that this 1940s-era passenger train ran along,
became the predecessor to many of the bike trails that exist today.

BICYCLE
SAFETY

BICYCLE SAFETY

Bicycling offers many rewards, among them a physically fit body and a pleasant means of transportation. But the sport has its hazards, which can lead to serious accidents and injuries. We have provided rules, facts and tips that can help minimize the dangers of bicycling while you're having fun.

CHOOSE THE RIGHT BICYCLE

Adults and children should ride bicycles with frames small enough to be straddled easily with both feet flat on the ground, and with handlebars that can be easily reached with elbows bent. Oversize bikes make it difficult to ride comfortably and maintain control. Likewise, don't buy a large bike for a child to grow into–smaller is safer.

LEARN TO RIDE THE SAFE WAY

When learning to ride a bike, let a little air out of the tires, and practice steering and balancing by "scootering" around with both feet on the ground and the seat as low as possible. The "fly-or-fall" method, where someone runs alongside the bicycle and then lets go, can result in injuries.

Training wheels don't work, because the rider can't learn to balance until the wheels come off. They can be used with a timid rider, but the child still will have to learn to ride without them. Once the rider can balance and pedal (without training wheels), raise the seat so that the rider's leg is almost straight at the bottom of the pedal stroke.

Children seldom appreciate the dangers and hazards of city cycling. Make sure they understand the traffic laws before letting them onto the road.

USE THIS IMPORTANT EQUIPMENT:

Headlight: A working headlight and rear reflector are required for night riding in some states. Side reflectors do not make the rider visible to drivers on cross streets.

Safety seat for children under 40 lbs.: Make sure the seat is mounted firmly over the rear wheel of the bike and does not wobble when going downhill at high speed. Make sure the child will not slide down while riding. The carrier should also have a device to keep the child's feet from getting into the spokes.

Package rack: Racks are inexpensive, and they let the rider steer with both hands and keep packages out of the spokes.

OBEY TRAFFIC LAWS

Car drivers are used to certain rules of the road, and bicyclists must obey them, too. The following rules should be taught to a child as soon as he or she can ride a bicycle:

Make eye contact with a driver before entering or crossing lanes.

Signal and glance over your shoulder before changing lanes.

Watch for openings in the traffic stream, and make turns from the appropriate lane.

When riding off-road, be sure you are on a trail that permits bicycles.

Before riding in the road, these rules should be practiced until they become habit and can be performed smoothly. Adults must set good examples; children imitate them regardless of verbal instructions.

BEWARE OF DANGEROUS PRACTICES

Never ride against traffic. Failure to observe this rule causes the majority of car-bicycle collisions. Motorists can't always avoid the maneuvers of a wrong-way rider, because the car and bike move toward each other very quickly.

Never make a left turn from the right lane.

Never pass through an intersection at full speed.

Never ignore stop lights or stop signs.

Never enter traffic suddenly from a driveway or sidewalk. This rule is particularly important when the rider is a child, who is more difficult for a motorist to see.

Don't wear headphones that make it hard to hear and quickly respond to traffic.

Don't carry passengers on a bike. The only exception is a child under 40 lbs. who is buckled into an approved bike safety seat and wears a helmet as required by law.

Passenger trailers can be safe and fun. Be aware, though, that a trailer makes the bike much longer and requires careful control. Passengers must wear helmets.

FIND SAFE PLACES TO RIDE

Most cities have some bicycle-friendly routes, as well as some high-traffic areas that require skill and experience. It's safest to ride on secondary roads with light traffic. When choosing a route, remember that the wider the lane, the safer the cycling.

GET A BIKE THAT WORKS WITH YOU

Skilled riders who use their bikes often for exercise or transport should consider buying multi-geared bikes, which increase efficiency while minimizing stress on the body. (These bikes may not be appropriate for young or unskilled riders, who may concentrate more on the gears than on the road.) The goal is to keep the pedals turning at a rate of 60-90 RPM. Using the higher gears while pedaling slowly is hard on the knees, and is slower and more tiring than the efficient pedaling on the experienced cyclist.

Have a safe trip!

Reprinted from July 1989 "Mayo Clinic Health Letter" with permission of Mayo Foundation, for Medical Education and Research, Rochester, Minnesota.

BICYCLE HELMETS

"It's as easy as falling off a bicycle." The adage has been around for decades. Unfortunately, it makes light of the potential for tragedy if you should take a serious fall while riding a bicycle.

With an increasing number of people riding bicycles on our streets and highways, the risk of injury, in particular, head injury, continues to rise. Each year, nearly 50,000 bicyclists suffer serious head injuries. According to the most recent statistics, head injuries are the leading cause of death in the approximately 1,300 bicycle-related fatalities that occur annually. To a large extent, these head injuries are preventable.

Wearing a helmet can make a difference. Until recently, advocates of the use of protective headgear for cyclists found their stance lacked scientific support. But wearing protective headgear clearly makes a difference. Recent evidence confirms that a helmet can reduce your risk of serious head and brain injury by almost 90 percent, should you be involved in a bicycle accident.

Bicycle riding is an excellent form of aerobic exercise that can benefit your musculoskeletal and cardiovascular systems. Make the investment in a helmet and take the time to put it on each time you ride.

WHAT TO LOOK FOR IN A BICYCLE HELMET:

We endorse these guidelines for bicycle helmets recommended by the American Academy of Pediatrics:

The helmet should meet the voluntary testing standards of one of these two groups: American National Standards Institute (ANSI) OR Snell Memorial Foundation. Look for a sticker on the inside of the helmet.

1) Select the right size. Find one that fits comfortably and doesn't pinch.

2) Buy a helmet with a durable outer shell and a polystyrene liner. Be sure it allows adequate ventilation.

3) Use the adjustable foam pads to ensure a proper fit at the front, back and sides.

4) Adjust the strap for a snug fit. The helmet should cover the top of your forehead and not rock side to side or back and forth with the chain strap in place.

5) Replace your helmet if it is involved in an accident.

A FEW MORE BIKE SAFETY TIPS

By Shawn E. Richardson

RAIL-TRAIL COURTESY & COMMON SENSE

1. Stay on designated trails.

2. Bicyclists use the right side of the trail; walkers use the left side of the trail.

3. Bicyclists should only pass slower users on the left side of the trail; use your voice to warn others when you need to pass.

4. Get off to the side of the trail if you need to stop.

5. Bicyclists should yield to all other users.

6. Do not use alcohol or drugs while on the trail.

7. Do not litter.

8. Do not trespass onto adjacent land.

9. Do not wear headphones while using the trail.

EMERGENCY TOOL-KIT

When venturing out on bicycle tours, it is always smart to take along equipment to help make roadside adjustments and repairs. It is not necessary for every member of your group to carry a complete set of equipment, but make sure someone in your group brings along the equipment listed below:

1. Standard or slotted screwdriver.

2. Phillips screwdriver.

3. 6" or 8" adjustable wrench.

4. Small pliers.

5. Spoke adjuster.

6. Tire pressure gauge.

7. Portable tire pump.

8. Spare innertube

9. Tire-changing lugs.

A FEW OTHER THINGS

When embarking on a extended bike ride, it is important to give your bike a pre- ride check. To ensure that your bike is in premium condition, go over the bike's mechanisms, checking for any mechanical problems. It's best to catch these at home, and not when they occur "on the road." If you run into a problem that you can't fix yourself, you should check your local yellow pages for a professional bike mechanic.

When you are planning a longer trip, be sure to consider your own abilities and limitations, as well as those of any companions who may be riding with you. In general, you can ride about three times the length (time-wise) as your average training ride. If you have a regular cycling routine, this is a good basis by which to figure the maximum distance you can handle.

Finally, be aware of the weather. Bring plenty of sun block for clear days, and rain gear for the rainy one. Rain can make some rides miserable, in addition to making it difficult to hear other traffic. Winds can blow up sand, and greatly increase the difficulty of a trail.

Most trails can be used for hiking as well as biking, like this person using the Heritage Rail-trail.

ABOUT THE AUTHOR

Shawn E. Richardson has worked as a cartographer for the Ohio Department of Transportation since 1988. He specializes in photogrammetry, the process of creating maps using aerial photography. He received his Bachelor of Science degree in environmental geography with emphasis on cartography from Kentucky's University of Louisville in 1985. A Kentucky native, Shawn has lived in Ohio since 1988.

Shawn enjoys bicycle touring, and his excursions can last anywhere from a few hours to several days. Although he has biked back roads through many states including Ohio's Tour of the Scioto River Valley, the majority of his touring has been on trails. He is an active member of the Rails-to-Trails Conservancy and has belonged to the Columbus Outdoor Pursuits, the American Youth Hostels and to the Louisville Wheelmen. This edition is the second major revision of Biking Ohio's Rail-Trails, Shawn's first book. If you have questions or comments for Shawn, you can contact him by writing to him in care of Biking U.S.A.'s Rail-Trails, P.O. Box 284, Hilliard, OH 43026-0284.

Author Shawn E. Richardson.